DEEP DIVE

JOSIAH VENTURE

©Copyright 2013 Josiah Venture

Josiah Venture
P.O. Box 4317
Wheaton, IL 60189-4317
(630) 221.9332
www.josiahventure.com

In partnership with
Dialogues In Action LLC
408 NW 12th Ave. Suite 506
Portland, OR 97209
www.dialoguesinaction.com

Special Thanks To

Brian Stephens
Deep Dive JV Project Coordinator

Dušan Drabina
Czech Republic Project Manager

Daniel Johnson
Czech Republic Project Author

Vahur Kobin
Estonia Project Manager

Innar Druglov
Estonia Project Author

Maruška Kožlejová
Slovakia Project Manager and Author

Josh Patty
Slovenia Project Manager and Author

Daniel Eifling
Poland Project Manager and Author

Ben and Kristy Williams
Ukraine Project Manager and Author

CONTENTS

Introduction
7

Slovania
9

Poland
25

Slovakia
55

Ukraine
79

Estonia
95

Czech Republic
111

Interview Protocols
137

INTRODUCTION

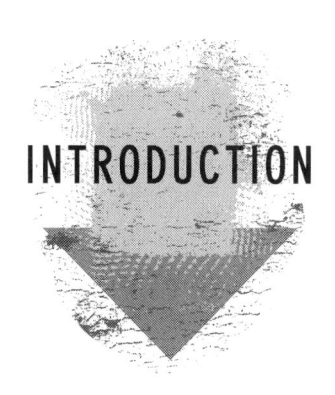

During 2012-2013, six teams of leaders from among the twelve national organizations of Josiah Venture serving the emerging generation in Eastern and Central Europe embarked on a qualitative study of their ministry environments.

Each team identified one critical obstacle to ministry fruitfulness. As a team and under the guidance of a researcher, they designed a qualitative research project to discover what they needed to know better and understand more fully. They took the issue that was most puzzling to them and set out to talk to people about it. Their aim was to gain fresh insight into their ministry environments and make progress on that one challenge, thereby increasing the fruitfulness of their ministry.

Doing good qualitative inquiry is not easy. The demands of ministry often afford little time for ministers to engage in meaningful conversations with people outside their immediate contexts of service. Also, being embedded in ministry over an extended period can make even the most astute leaders fail to notice some of the subtle but meaningful shifts in their surrounding human context. Recognizing these tendencies, the Josiah Venture teams set out to take a fresh, disciplined, and rigorous look at their ministry

INTRODUCTION

environments. They wanted to focus attention anew on the people they are called to serve.

Here's the context: Josiah Venture (JV) started with three couples in 1993 and a vision to see "a movement of God among the youth of Central and Eastern Europe that finds its home in the local church and transforms society." Today, over 200 staff members and hundreds of additional volunteers and partners are joined in the ministry in 12 countries. Over half of the JV staff members are nationals. They are supported by teams in North America and Canada.

Thousands of young leaders are trained each year in the ministries of JV, and through these hundreds of new believers are being discipled in the local church. But the ministry leaders of JV desire to see increasing spiritual fruit in and through young followers of Christ. They desire to see their ministries produce fruit of quality that will last. Increased fruitfulness depends in part upon an understanding of who is being sought, how they think, what drives them, how they run their lives, what is keeping them from growing, and what is in their hearts.

Over the course of the Deep Dive Project, 90 youth leaders conducted 422 in-depth interviews with youth and youth leaders in Slovenia, Estonia, Czech Republic, Poland, Ukraine, and Slovakia.[1] Their objective was to see more clearly and understand more deeply the youth and youth leaders they serve.

This book is about what they discovered.

---

[1] The teams followed a modified process of qualitative research, including the following components: Team training in qualitative ideas, Design of interview protocol by the team (see appendix), Identification of population and sample, Interview and data gathering technique, Individual analysis, Group analysis, Response for signature programs, Design of innovation experiments.

DEEP
DIVE
8

JV SLOVENIA

How do Slovene youth engage in groups?

David Bordner, Katka Bordner, Sebastian Forjan, Gloria Forjan, Terry Jackson, Lori Jackson, Mateja Jagodic, Brad Jenkins, Laurel Jenkins, Shauna Kopra, Andrej Lovše, Nina Lovše, Matt Mormance, Sharon Mormance, Josh Patty, Kristi Patty, Sephanie Rogers, Johnny Stevens, Brooke Stevens, Hondo Wynn, Trish Wynn

The Josiah Venture (JV) team in Slovenia has been engaging the emerging generation of young people with the gospel of Christ for over a decade now. Presently, 26 staff—both North Americans and Slovenes—serve full-time on this team. Our mission is to fan into flame a movement of God among the youth of Slovenia.

Slovenia is a beautiful and unique country. It also has one of the smallest Evangelical populations in the world. Operation World, a global mission research publication, ranks Slovenia 14th in the world for the smallest percentage of Evangelical believers per capita. That percentage is worse than Iraq, Iran, and most every African nation. There is an acute need to evangelize young people, connect them to Christian groups, and mobilize them to reach their peers.

Great strides have been made to evangelize young people, establish vibrant youth ministries, and involve the emerging generation in the local church. Still, some cultural aspects have been puzzling. One of the most vexing relates to the ways that youth in Slovenia engage the Christian youth group.

Most youth ministry models from the West are based on the assumption that young people will be attracted to peers through some form of youth group. In Slovenia, relationships have been quick to be established one-on-one, but less easily through youth groups. And yet, Slovene youth often belong to groups and exhibit durable commitment to groups, just not the kind of youth groups the JV team has been offering.

To understand and respond to the unique cultural expressions of the Slovene context, we launched our Deep Dive project to answer the question,

How are Slovene youth drawn to and engage in groups?

Twenty-one of our staff members conducted 93 in-depth interviews with Slovene youth. Based on the findings, we adjusted our signature programs and designed entirely new ministry initiatives. A number of themes emerged from the data corpus. We translated the themes into findings to capture the main ideas in a memorable and meaningful form. The most salient are rendered here:

Finding 1
What motivates initial participation in a group?

There were two outstanding motivations for initially joining a Slovene group - The opportunity for self improvement and the promise of measurable impact on society.

The opportunity for self-improvement

In Slovene society, initial participation in a group most often begins with an opportunity for self-improvement. Slovenes will join a group because they want to learn a new skill or further develop their abilities. We saw a number of teens involved in groups focused on Karate, soccer, dance, and music. This might seem identical to a North American free-time activity, but the groups took on a significantly different flavor. The groups were not for the purpose of recreation, but for the purpose of self improvement and future success. If you were involved in music, you were likely training to be a professional musician. If you played soccer, you were on a feeder team attached to a professional or semi-professional club. Anyone there for "just the fun of it" was quickly shown the door. The level of commitment required to excel in a given activity means that there typically isn't time to be a part of more than one group. The goal is often to master a given skill rather than be a "jack of all trades."

We observed this motivation for self improvement coming inpart from a fear of insignificance and irrelevance. Youth are defining "Who am I?" externally. Self-improvement provides a sense of security for the future and a sense of personal significance. The group setting not only provides a context for personal development but also provides a stage for recognizing an individual's success. The most successful groups often have clear means of measuring and recognizing personal achievement. Someone involved in music or dance hold public recitals in prominent locations. Even "kiddie" ballet has their recital in the national ballet theater. Musicians perform biannually before a panel of judges who grad them. These grades determined if they can continue in the program. The martial arts track seems particularly noteworthy as teens worked their way up through each color of belt. It is also interesting to us that upon reaching the highest level of achievement within a group, many then left the group for another. (For example, many youth left Karate after achieving the black belt.)

The promise of measurable impact on society

Another overriding motivation for joining a group is the promise of having measurable impact on society. This more altruistic motivation pervaded even organizations like dance clubs. One member reflected, "It meant so much to us that our dance troop was serving the nation by preserving and demonstrating our cultural heritage." Slovenes are much more likely to join a group if they believed it will have a global impact. The opportunity to serve a higher cause justifies the time and sacrifice involved in participating in the group. In interviews, we noticed a sense of embarrassment if the group or activity was "just something they enjoyed." There needs to be the component of "this is making a difference for others" or "this is helping me improve" in order for them to feel comfortable participating over the long term.

Meaning and Implications

In contrast to this, our team had been employing an entirely differnt stategy for attracting people to our groups. We were adverstising a group where they would have fun and enjoy deep relationships. We still believe that these are things that Slovenes desire; but those desires are secondary. When faced with their demanding schedules, our groups have been the first to be shelved or dropped because they are not a high priority. Time and again, we have watched students visit our groups, say they absolutely love it, only to have them stop coming in a couple of weeks because of "lack of time." This same student would then train for two hours, five nights a week, with a karate group. He admitted that it wasn't very fun and that he didn't have a single friend in the group.

Finding 2
What fosters long term commitment to a group?

As we conducted our research, we observed that, for some groups, people were willing to sacrifice enormous amounts of time and exhibited a high level of commitment to the group. This was not true with many of our groups. We endeavored to discover what elements fostered such commitment to a group. The following are some of the components that we observed in successful Slovene groups.

Goal oriented

A group with clear goals offers a sense of safety and purpose and creates a greater level of commitment for Slovene participants. Goals are either a project or an end product. They desire that something tangible be created from the group. They are most responsive to a product of value that is recognized outside of the group and in the community. These take the form of regular sports competitions, music recitals, dance performances, service projects, and volunteer fire rallies.

We noticed that these goals and projects are best with short-term objectives that are attainable, potentially seasonal, and repetitive. This allows students to commit more easily since it is for a determined amount of time.

Role clarity and progression

In Slovene society, the concept of having a role within a group is important to consider and understand. Even minor roles count and help build longevity by giving a "place" within the group. Though some see simple participation as their role, many feel a sense of belonging if they can influence (contribute to) the group in a specific manner.

A few key elements became apparent in the research: First, the role does not need to be a leadership position. In fact, while many Slovenes (especially guys) want a specific role, they usually do not want the position of leader. Second, we noticed that youth in this culture will thrive when given specific and clear responsibilities for their role. A teen believes, "If I know exactly what to do and what is expected of me, then I won't fail." And finally, they are motivated by a progression of roles and/or training within a group. This anticipation of a future role provides incentive for participation and commitment. We saw this at work particularly strongly in the Catholic youth system. Students were extremely committed, not because of a belief system, but because of a role hierarchy that they were working their way up.[1]

Defining experiences

Whenever we found high commitment to a specific group, we usually found stories of defining moments that sealed their loyalty. Often this was an experience outside the normal routine of the group, most notably through trips together (for example, choir tour, vacationing together, service projects, special road trip, etc)

Finding 3
When do Slovenes join a group?

We discovered that the culture is not transient in nature. In other words, they are unlikely to move from group to group. In addition, they typically dedicate most of their time to one or, at the most, two groups. We noticed that most join their groups

---

[1] Note of contrast – With existing leaders we were trying to cover all of the "busy work" so that our Slovene leaders had time to invest in relationships. This had the effect of making them feel on the outside because they didn't have a visible tangible role. As hard as we tried we couldn't get our leaders to engage in relational ministry. When we reversed this and gave them all of the "menial" tasks, we found them owning the group and engaging heavily in relationship building.

in elementary school, or in the gap years between elementary and high school and between high school and college. (There is no middle school in Slovenia.) We saw that high-school teens in grades 11-13 had already chosen their groups and were much less likely to join a new group even if it was attractive. The implications for our team is that we need to focus our primary contact ministries at the upper-elementary level (ages 12-14) if we hope to have them engaged in a high school group in the future.

An example of the perfect Slovene Group: The Volunteer Fire Brigade

One of the things that prompted our study was comparing our struggles with the huge success of the "Gasilci" or volunteer fire brigades. In some villages up to 30% of the total population is a member of the Gasilci. Within these volunteer organizations we see all the components of our research.

The opportunity for self-improvement. From age 8 to 80 participants are trained in new skills and stretched physically.

The promise of measurable impact on society. Being a part of a group that saves live, protects property, and invests in the community, which is a huge draw in this culture. The fire brigades also organize the main town celebrations (fun) which everyone attends and supports because "it is for a good cause".

Goal oriented. Each fire club is regularly working towards or training for fire competitions with other clubs. They do this in addition to regular performance reviews and certification tests. This inspires a deep level of member commitment and camaraderie.

Role clarity and progression. Each participant is given very clear roles and tasks within the club. Success takes the form of "ranks" which every person earns in military fashion. With these ranks come leadership and training responsibilities. The organization is broken into a large number of squads in order to provide lots of opportunities for engagement and upward mobility within the group.

Defining experiences. The group will often travel together, compete together, and organize the key social gatherings for the local community.

In a nut shell, the Gasilci are the secular version of what we wish for the Church to be in a given community.

Renovation of Signature Programs

We desire to apply the findings to the current programs, to renovate them in response to what we have discovered through the inquiry. In particular we are applying the findings to three signature programs:

Youth Group

Our current model of "youth groups" focus on forming an alternative community of Slovene youth that develops healthy relationships, provides fun, and offers the chance to be mentored by a mature Christian and learn about God. These groups typically meet weekly where we play a few fun or relational games, give a prepared talk, and informally enjoy food and each other's company. The leaders usually plan and execute a monthly fun event and seek to meet with the students individually in hopes of developing a mentorship relationship. The primary focus in these groups is the relational aspect.

Goal Oriented. We have learned that our groups need to have specific and obtainable goals that we can work toward together. This will help build relationships within the group. In response, we are guiding ourselves by the assumption that working toward a goal outside the group will help form the inside of the group (for example, service projects, mission trips, helping in one specific area of town, serve at English camp, or help younger kids).

Self-Improvement. Our youth groups strive to improve the lives of our students. We know that Jesus, through the counsel of the Holy Spirit is really the only way we can truly improve as people. This is the "self- improvement" we offer our students. This is a real need, which is often not a felt need. Our research shows that Slovenes desire to gain experiences and skills in life that will help them become more marketable and well-rounded people. Our youth groups need to focus more on offering to meet the felt needs of our students, giving them opportunity to progress as they develop specific skills. These ideas are based on the assumption that offering ways to help students improve their life will improve the group: learning specific skills such as photography, video recording, cooking, event-planning, skiing/snowboarding, or playing a musical instrument. Also we want to be intentional about helping to develop life skills: conflict resolution, financial planning, job skills, time management, relationships, public speaking, peer crisis, or dealing with parents.

Roles. Our research shows that Slovenes feel significant and helpful if they are given responsibility and have a specific role within a group. This increases regular participation. If there is one leader of the group who is doing everything, the group will not function best. Our motto should be: "every student has a role." Even simple, mundane roles are important and should be given to students. The leader should not be doing most of what needs to be done in order for the group to function. Ideas are as follows: clean up crew, welcoming crew (slippers, coffee, tea offered), create face book events, organize or bring food, or help with planning.

Camp

English camps are designed to provide quality English instruction in an environment where relationships are formed for the purpose of exposing teenagers to the claims of Christ.

Native speaking English teachers and high school students from a church in America join Slovene churches to provide a week-long camp experience. English classes are held each morning, the afternoon is dedicated to relaxation and activities by interest (sports, crafts, music), and the evenings include a talk and discussion about developmentally appropriate life issues.

We are applying the findings from this research in English Camps in these ways:

Specific Roles. Slovenes value clear and defined role progression within a group; this provides group members with significance and security. Because of the numerous responsibilities at camp, this is an excellent opportunity to engage as many of the core students in running the camp. It requires extra initial effort and planning, but will serve to create much stronger commitment to the group. Even the new students could be given roles within their small group class. They could be given the role of class recorder, timekeeper, game leader, debate organizer.

Opportunity for self-improvement and clear goals. These give purpose and/or even excuse for joining a group. The best goal for the Slovene group is in short-term situations that are attainable, potentially seasonal, and repetitive. Since the goal or project has limited time, it allows students to commit more easily. A common goal gives a sense of belonging and leads to stronger relationships.

It is important for us to emphasize the goal of learning English. We can use this to our advantage. This element of camps can be highlighted especially in promotion and follow-up with educators, students, and parents. Even though it might feel like school, a progress report, certificate of completion, and a performance for the parents could be powerful tools for motivating and recognizing participation in the program.

Defining experiences. We need to help individual teachers at creating more than just a class, but a tight-knit group. This might require thinking "outside the box" (for example, skipping an hour of class and going out for ice cream, "sneaking" out for a midnight swim together, challenging another class to a competition, pulling off a surprise party for someone at camp, etc.) Anything to help the group feel like they have experienced something unique together would be helpful. This could be a new training module for pre-camp training or an orientation to inspire teachers and staff in how they can make a lasting difference in the lives of Slovene students.

Pala (Performing Arts)

The intended impact of the Pala is to share the love of Christ to lost high school students through music and drama. Music is a key influencer in the life of every teenager. What they believe, how they act, and what they value is shaped and impacted by the music they listen to. The program of Pala is specifically designed to bring the message of the gospel into the heart and life of teenagers through excellence, community, and God.

Much of the research validates the unique ministry and strategy of Pala. While there were still areas that were lacking, much of what PALA does fits with what we have found to be true of Slovene youth. A few of the things that PALA is doing well is including elements of self-improvement, community, and clear goals.

One of the ways that PALA is lacking is in the ownership of the group and in providing opportunities for young people to rise to leadership roles.

One of the first things we changed as a result of this research was giving more leadership (or more clearly defined roles) to the current leaders. As a result there has been a huge impact on the leaders' posture and attitude towards the group and their involvement. We have seen a monumental change in the culture of the group and in the involvement of the leaders. When they had clear roles and specific tasks they were much more likely to engage in the "relational" component of outreach. This was opposite of our initial strategy. We worked hard to take care of many of the details so that our student leaders would have time to invest relationally in other students. But we found that as their responsibilities increased, so did their ownership and willingness to reach out to others.

There are a variety of ways in which leaders are trained and developed. There are three leaders who are a part of the leadership team and are involved in the big picture of the group. Each of them is in a role that will stretch his or her abilities without sacrificing quality in the group. There are also a variety of roles held by other students (writing dramas, creating and teaching choreography, and leading sectionals, picking out songs). These provide ownership and an avenue to express their talents.

Design of Experiments

The approach we have taken to design new programs has been to identify a number of experiments. Instead of to seeking to develop the single "silver bullet," our approach to program innovation is to construct six experiments to test the application of these ideas in various ways and in various areas of the ministry. Experiments are designed to be modest so that they are not distracting from the main work, time-bound so that we can learn quickly from them, multiple and simultaneous so that they are properly experimental and not churning the attention and focus of the staff. Experiments are meant to fail without compromising our effectiveness. We intend to learn from our failures. Others will succeed; we will build on those.

Based on our findings, we have designed six experiments that we will run in the next nine months of ministry activity. Below is a short summary of these experiments

Experiment 1 – Teen crisis first responders program

This experiment will consist of a weekend training for teen leaders to recognize the signs of common crisis situations amongst their peers (suicide, addictions, abuse, eating disorders) and give them tools for assessing the threat and getting them the help they need. We will involve Christian counselors and medical professionals from around the country. This program touches on the desire for self improvement, measurable impact on society, and goal oriented aspects of our findings. If successful, this is a possible program to offer to schools as a regular program to train young leaders and those most likely to be "first on the scene."

Experiment 2 – English club/Matura prep

Since education is so valuable in our country, we wanted to come up with a way to help students perform well in school. We want to jump on board with the teachers and find a way to come alongside of high school students that begin to worry about the Matura test before they even start their freshman year!

We plan to start with a 3-month trial of a club version of a language school, where we would teach students English, play games with them, talk to them about life and also provide some basic studying skills, help them with their oral exams and provide support as they are trying to navigate high school.

Experiment 3 - Creative Arts Training: Video Contest

This program would be designed to create a place for teenagers to work together to accomplish a common goal and showcase their creativity in a public forum. Each team will create a 60 second video answering the question: "How has English Camp changed your life?" Videos will be posted to the English camp Facebook page where they will be shared with friends and liked.

Two valuable prizes will be given in both group and individual categories—viewers' choice (based upon Facebook likes) and editors' choice (chosen by a panel of judges based upon creativity).

We will offer a prize for the winner and showcase the created work on a large stage. There will be roles throughout the creation of the videos, recognizing that these videos serve a larger purpose will provide a place where the students have influence on a larger scale. Sharing the impact that English camp has had in their life and hearing the stories of others will help participants to see that they are a part of a larger body of people who are involved in English camps. The pilot will run during the first two weeks of June and will target the social network of students who have been involved in English camps in the past.

Experiment 4 – Fusion

As soon as we began our research it became apparent that Fusion choirs were going to be one of our most effective tools for engaging these cultural motivations that were uncovered. We asked for an accelerated launch of fusion in Celje and are preparing to launch another in Maribor as soon as possible.

Experiment 5 – Sports Training/tournament

In our desire to reach young men we plan to capitalize on the fact that we have ministries in several different cities. We are organizing a weekend, nation-wide, paintball tournament, preceded by training events in individual communities on tactics, battle, manhood, and teamwork. We hope to take advantage of the desire to compete, learn a new skill, and improve. If successful, this could be developed into a sport league (possibly for other sports like baseball, dodge ball, etc.)

Experiment 6 – Social entrepreneurship

We would like to provide training and create a club/learning community that would focus on business entrepreneurship in addition to social responsibility. We would like to create a place where young leaders could be trained in servant leadership, ethical business, and societal impact within the marketplace.

JV POLAND

What is the road to becoming a youth ministry "motor" in the emerging generation in Poland?

Daniel Eifling, Michal Skiba, Iwona Eifling, Piotr Dymkowski,
Laura Hash, Dan Hash, Dawid Werner, Susan Ellis,
Greg Carlson, Marcin Bista, Lukasz Kropisz

Where are the young leaders in youth ministry in Poland? Who will lead the next generation? Are the young leaders from within this new generation qualitatively different than those of the previous generation? If leaders from within the emerging generation are active in ministry, have they been identified, equipped and empowered, or did they find their way alone? Who are they, what are they like, and how did they become people of influence in their generation? These are the questions Stowarzyszenie Fala has been wrestling with over the past year.

Stowarzyszenie Fala (Fala for short, which means "wave" in Polish) is a Polish national partner organization of Josiah Venture. We have been developing youth ministry in Poland informally for 20 years, and formally as an association for 10 years through evangelism, discipleship and youth ministry training. Fala partners with local churches to support and empower their work of reaching youth with the gospel. We offer language camps, music and sports ministries, and prevention workshops in local schools.

In addition to evangelism, Fala helps youth ministries disciple young people. We equip young leaders through conferences and camps, ministry resources, training programs and mentoring. We believe that everything we do in Fala must cause the local church to prosper, and that leaders who are transformed into the image of Christ will transform the world around them. We have ministry programs which develop youth ministry broadly and across all denominations. While we serve the movement of youth ministry nationally, each of our workers also serves in a local church. This helps each of us experience the same joys and sorrows that are locally experienced by the youth leaders.

Over the past few years we have noticed a significant change in youth ministry leadership. It appears there is a lack of young leaders coming out of the emerging generation. Cultural and generational changes as well as challenges confronting the church have led to the emergence of a different type of leader in this generation. They have different needs, priorities, motivations and visions of youth ministry than those held by the previous generation. As a youth ministry training organization that desires to come alongside churches and reach the next generation by equipping its leaders, we have needed a better understanding of the leaders in the emerging generation. To this end, Fala conducted a qualitative research study of young leaders in youth ministry from among the emerging generation in Poland.

Through in-depth conversations with young leaders, we sought to understand how they grew into the kind of people who were not only influencing youth but were "motors," driving youth ministry forward in Poland today. We began with the awareness that not all formal youth leaders are "motors," and not all "motors" are formal youth leaders. Therefore, for the purpose of our study we chose to use the word "motor" rather than "leader" to identify these young people. With that in mind, the goal of our study was to find the answer to the question:

What is the road to becoming a motor in youth ministry in the emerging generation in Poland?

With an answer to this question, we believe Fala, as well as other church and para-church organizations in Poland, will be able to identify, equip, and empower these motors to "go and make disciples" (Matthew 28:19-20) among the youth of Poland.

We interviewed 66 motors in youth ministry from January to March, 2013. Interviews were led by 11 employees of Fala and were done face-to-face or via Skype (with only a couple exceptions). Each interview lasted from 45 to 90 minutes. Among the motors interviewed, 32 were women and 34 were men. Their ages ranged from 17 to 31 years. Motors were involved in either para-church youth ministry or church youth ministry (from Baptist, Brethren, Chrystusowy, Evangelical Free, Pentecostal, Lutheran, Non-Denominational, and Roman Catholic churches).

Stowarzyszenie Fala engaged this study for three reasons:

First, we want our ministry to be more effective. We need to learn from the ones we serve in order to better serve them. The meaning and implications for ministry sections in the following discussion apply to both our broad national youth ministry programs as well as our ministries in local churches. Both are vital aspects of our ministry of training leaders. We've written in the first person, and the "we" refers to Fala and its workers both in their local church ministries and in national programs.

Second, we found that those we interviewed are true motors. These were not just random people involved in youth ministry.

These young people are actively involved and fruitful in youth ministry, have true influence on the young generation, and are often identified as motors not only by those in Fala, but by their peers, priests and pastors, and other motors.

Third, the findings in this study flow directly from what the motors in Poland shared with us about their journey to becoming a motor. We are attempting to give them a voice. As we analyzed the data from the interviews with the 66 motors, we consistently saw six key themes which help us answer the question, "What is the road to becoming a motor in youth ministry in the emerging generation in Poland?" As we listen to their voice and learn from them, our hope is that we will be more prepared to raise up a wave of leaders in the next generation to fulfill the Great Commission in Poland.

Finding 1
Calling

Looking at the ministry landscape in Poland, it would be easy to assume that there is a shortage of young leaders called to youth ministry. A majority of churches don't have a formally-led youth ministry. In the churches where there is a traditional youth group, the leader is a young person who was appointed by the pastor or priest or elected by the youth group. They have little to no experience, training, or education. In addition, evangelical seminaries are experiencing low numbers of traditional students. With these symptoms, it would be easy to conclude that there are no young people who have a calling to serve in youth ministry.

What causes this lack of young leaders who are called to ministry? Is it the fault of youth who are no longer committed to serving God because of the influence of culture, materialism and ever-increasing academic, financial and career opportunities? Or does the fault lie with the church which, as some might say, may be failing to raise up leaders in this young generation?

While there may be anecdotal evidence to support both of these assertions, our research points to a third option. In our conversations with motors, we clearly saw that it was a deep sense of calling which leads them to serve in youth ministry. However, this generation has a very different understanding of calling than its predecessors.

Process of Discovery

In answer to our research question, "What is the road to becoming a motor in youth ministry in Poland," we found that this generation overwhelmingly experiences calling as a process of discovery, not as a one-time event. Very few of the motors we interviewed had the experience of God revealing their calling in a single moment. Motors consistently said that their sense of a call was an unfolding journey of discovery.

One of the benefits of interviewing 66 motors is that we could hear how people in different places on the road to becoming a motor spoke about calling. Consistently, people near the beginning of their journey wouldn't even use the word calling. It's as if it were too big of a word. Although using different vocabulary, they were still essentially describing calling. "I serve in spite of many difficulties because I have a sense of responsibility before God for these youth," explained a 19 year-old girl from the Pentecostal church. A 23 year-old Catholic girl said, "I became aware that no one in my church was telling teenagers that God loves them and wants to have a living relationship with them. I decided I had to do something." Another motor said, "I have a burning passion in my heart to see revival in my generation." Using words like responsibility, duty, and burning passion, these young motors described how they are compelled to serve God from a deep inner motivation. In contrast, motors further down the road used the word "calling" more easily. They had grown into the awareness that they are called to youth ministry.

Essence over Form or Role

Another defining aspect is that this young generation has a broader understanding of calling. The essence of their calling is more important than the form, position, role or location of their ministry. Motors frequently made statements like, "I'm called to love people and make disciples. Today that may be in youth ministry and in a few years that might be as a small group leader."

Duration of Calling

The third important aspect to how motors understand calling is that it can be temporary. One motor said, "This is my place for now." Another said, "I'm sure God wants me to do this for now." Out of the 66 motors we interviewed, only a couple talked about calling like one 31 year-old youth leader from Warsaw, "It wasn't until I got a ways into my youth ministry that I understood this is my calling. Now I want to be a youth leader all of my life." Overwhelmingly, motors see their calling as temporary. They seemed to say, "If life circumstances change, or my passions change, I can move on to something else." We could interpret this negatively, as if this generation won't commit to anything; however, the heart of the motors we spoke with was more focused on the urgency to live their passions in the time they have now. Living in a world of constant change (technology, economy, etc.), they are focused on what they can do here and now for God because at any moment life can change. While there may be many in this generation who avoid commitments and responsibility, one of the defining characteristics of motors is this sense of "making the most of the time we have." It is an admirable quality which could be misconstrued or misunderstood.

Meaning and Implications

They Are Called, But What Is a Calling?

So what does this mean for training leaders among this and future generations? First, there's good news: God is calling young men and women to reach the youth of Poland! However, these leaders understand and experience their calling differently, and function in it differently, than previous generations. Motors in this young generation experience calling as a process of discovery rather than an event. The motors we interviewed consistently communicated that this discovery happened over the course of many years.

There is also a different vocabulary to describe calling. We might erroneously conclude that some are not called to ministry because of the words they use when in fact they are. Another danger is that if they don't fit into "our mold" of calling, these young motors will be under-utilized or take their gifts and passions and apply them elsewhere. If we restrict our definition of calling to a specific task, job or role, we might miss the heart of this generation. They tend to understand calling more broadly as loving God, loving others, and making disciples. Are we willing to create a path toward leadership, and change the vocabulary we use to accommodate their experience of calling and to engage motors more effectively?

For the purposes of this study, we have withheld judgment on whether the experience of calling described by many motors in this generation is Biblical or not (or for that matter, whether or not "our" typical experience and theology is completely Biblical). That was not the task of this research. Further work needs to be done. For both our generation and theirs, we need to sort out how much of the experience and understanding of calling is based on culture, generational factors and changes, or even reaction to societal and church experiences. Rather than an "us vs. them" mentality, how can the older and younger generation stand side-by-side, look at Biblical texts, and together form a more full and complete theology of calling? While experience can inform our theology, both generations need to critique their existing theology in light of scripture and refine theology and interpret experience in light of the truth of God's word.

A Ministry Greenhouse

We learned much from mentors about the kind of environment they need in order to discover their calling. Motors need a safe environment in which they can "test the waters" of ministry. From the data, we learned that this "safe environment" is characterized by:

- a low commitment level at the very beginning with increasing degrees of commitment over time
- clear and realistic expectations,
- an adequate amount of time and space to grow and discover their calling, talents and skills, and heart for youth, and
- support from a loving relationship with a mentor or leader.

These qualities created a sort of "greenhouse" for motors to discover their calling and commit more and more deeply to youth ministry. The motors which were thriving in their ministries were given the freedom and space they needed to travel step-by-step down the road to becoming the motor they are today.

From Temporary Ministry to Longevity in Ministry

Recognizing that their experience of calling is temporary does not mean that motors in this generation do not desire longevity in ministry. They do. But their path to longevity is different than what we thought. We must give motors the freedom to get involved slowly, incrementally, and progressively. We must simultaneously have the goal of longevity in mind and immediate, concrete steps which lead to a path of longevity. As we see in our other findings, personal challenges from trusted leadership and experiencing fruit in their ministries are keys to keep motors enduring in ministry. These propel them forward in their understanding of their calling.

That being said, not all motors will serve-long term. We must examine our motives. Do we only invest in leaders so that they will become full-time youth leaders? These young leaders we invest in and train up, both in our local churches and in Fala, do not belong to us or our local church or parachurch ministry, they belong to God. They are servants in His kingdom. As we invest in their development, we should not consider it a failure but a success if they serve in our youth ministries for a time and then take that leadership experience and ability and apply it in some other ministry or in their everyday life as a living witness for Jesus in their homes, schools, jobs and cities.

Finding 2
Personal Challenge to Ministry

If motors describe their experience of calling as a process of discovery, what is the catalyst that initiated that process? We tend to assume that if someone truly is a motor, they will find the way on their own. They will take the initiative to find their place in ministry. On the other extreme, we tend to assume that through extensive training or theological education someone will become a leader.

Challenged By Whom?

The motors we interviewed said that there was nearly always

an invitation to ministry or a challenge from someone to meet a need, which initiated the process and propelled them forward in discovering their calling. This challenge did not flow from the pulpit, but came directly from someone with whom they had a close relationship (their priest or pastor, youth leader, parent, uncle, etc.). What moved them to action was not only the challenge. It was someone who knew and loved them, identified potential in them, and intentionally communicated that they are needed and can contribute.

This challenge and invitation to ministry was critical because motors, due to either humility or insecurity (or both), didn't often see themselves as motors. One 19 year-old girl said, "I always wanted to serve God, but I waited until someone invited me before I began to get involved." Stepping up to the challenge helped them begin to see themselves the way others saw them, as valuable for God's work and as having something unique to contribute.

Challenged To What?

To what were they most often challenged? Often a trusted leader or authority challenged them to get involved in ministry to fill a specific role, meet a specific need, or reach a certain goal or cause. In other cases the personal challenge came to utilize specific gifts or talents to glorify God and serve Him.

While a personal challenge to ministry was often the catalyst to begin serving, motors said that challenges also played a key role throughout their development as leaders. At the beginning, challenges were primarily task-oriented and characterized by small, safe steps into ministry. With each "success" came increasing opportunities, responsibility and increasingly more invitations to serve. Later down the road of ministry, challenges kept motivating them to continue to serve faithfully. Without consistently receiving new levels of leadership in ministry and new roles which challenged them to grow as ministers and be dependent on God, motors said that they lost motivation to serve.

While a majority of motors we interviewed received this personal challenge, those that did not somehow took the initiative on their own to seek out ministry opportunities. They bemoaned that they had not receive this personal invitation to ministry, however. It was a major obstacle that they had to overcome in order to find a place in ministry. As much as the personal invitation to ministry motivated motors, receiving no challenge or support left them feeling demotivated, demoralized, and impotent. In many instances they described not only a lack of invitation or challenge, but an explicit or implicit message that young people don't have much to offer. One motor stated, "Churches don't respect or value young people. They expect youth to be there, but don't think youth have much to offer."

Meaning and Implications for Ministry

The Challenger

It is incredibly meaningful when the challenge or invitation to ministry comes from someone who is in a close personal relationship with the motor, and who will continuously shepherd and care for them. This close shepherding relationship is critical because it communicates how valuable the person is. The message that someone believes in these motors gives them courage and strengthens their faith. It helps them trust that God can use them. Also, without this intimate relationship and knowledge of the potential motor, we can misjudge their level of development and fall prey to one of the many dangers.

Dangers In Giving Challenges

We tend to go to one of two extremes in our invitations to ministry. We either (a) throw young motors into the deep end, placing everything on their shoulders at once, or (b) fail to actually empower them to do challenging and meaningful work for the Lord. In the first situation, the motors become overwhelmed. In the other, the motors become discouraged and full of self-doubt, questioning whether they are called or capable. On the road to becoming a motor in youth ministry, young people need appropriate challenges at the appropriate time.

Another major error we make is to view this personal challenge as no more than delegating tasks. The true value of a personal challenge to ministry is not primarily to accomplish tasks. The true value is the investment in developing of young leaders who will have incredible influence on God's kingdom. These investments demand much of us. But they will also produce exponentially more fruit.

Head, Hands and Heart Challenges

If our goal is to invite young people to ministry by challenging them to increasing involvement and leadership, the challenges we give them should not simply be task-oriented. In one voice, motors communicated that they are longing to grow holistically. Certainly, they need challenges to grow in their knowledge and skills in ministry. But more than that, these developing leaders need and crave challenges which touch their character, their hearts, and draw them deeper to faith and trust in God. Doing comes out of being. Above all else, in these invitations to ministry in the context of loving and trusting relationships, we must challenge these young leaders not only to do the work of the ministry, but to become motors shaped into the image of Christ.

Stair-Step Challenges

Growing to become a motor in youth ministry is clearly a journey along a road, or a path, but it also has a "stair-step" nature. Motors need repeated and ongoing challenges. They are motivated by ever-increasing levels of leadership. No matter what the ministry—youth ministry, children's ministry or as a small group leader—we need to provide motors in this generation with a path of growing leadership. Then need to be able to see which "stair-step" they are on as well as see where they are going next. We need to have a practical strategy in place which helps motors know when it's time for the next level of leadership, what the next level is, and what the mechanisms are to help catapult them to the next level of leadership. Important steps in their leadership development can begin with task-oriented roles but must move on to personal evangelism, peer care, co-leading, leading and then reproducing and multiplying.

One motor described moving through these exact "stair steps" through his participation in annual summer mission trips with "Generacja T". He explained, "Seven years ago I was cleaning toilets and playing with children. Then I got to share my testimony and be in dramas and skits. After that I became an assistant team leader, and for the past two years I've been a team leader with my own assistant and team." This motor had a clear path of ever-increasing leadership responsibility. There were mechanisms put in place by the organization which helped him move through these steps. He is now multiplying leaders at age 21 not only on mission trips but also in his local church.

Motors communicated that sometimes they can get "stuck" in one level of leadership, or on one stair-step. It's key to understand that motors do not "automatically" move from one step to the next. While we have the responsibility to create this path of growing leadership, motors also consistently described how God allowed natural challenges, trials and difficulties to catapult them to the next step. We who mentor and train motors must be sensitive to the work of the Holy Spirit in their lives and to what God desires to accomplish in them through the circumstances of their lives. This brings us full-circle to the unavoidable fact that motors

DEEP DIVE
37

need us to be involved in the intimate aspects of their lives, shepherding and caring for them. Without this relationship and sensitivity to the work of the Spirit, all of our strategy might be for naught.

Finding 3
Fruit in Ministry

In light of our research we are compelled to ask ourselves these questions: When we think of fruit in ministry, what comes to mind? Do we think of the number of participants? Or do we think of how many people have put their faith in Christ this year? How does the presence of fruit in ministry, or the lack of it impact us? The young people in our study explained that the idea of fruit in their ministry served a couple of very important roles. Equally intersting, though, was the kind of fruit they described.

Role of Fruit in Ministry

Motors in youth ministry described how fruit both revealed their calling and helped them endure faithfully in their calling despite difficulties. Over and over again, motors reported being certain of their calling because they see fruit in their ministry, when they see God using them. In fact, we consistently heard how one of the most discouraging things in ministry for motors was a lack of visible fruit. "Sometimes the only thing that keeps me going is the hope of seeing the fruit of my labor," one young motor said. Motors need to see the kind of measurable impact they are having. When they see fruit in their ministry, as another explained, "that is when I know that God is using me and that what I'm doing has meaning."

Important Types of Fruit for Motors

Fruit External to Themselves. We heard motors describe two types of fruit. The first was fruit in the lives of people in their ministry. We found it interesting that while a few focused on numbers, most emphasized life transformation.

> - **Evangelistic fruit:** "I'm very motivated by people coming to faith in Christ, especially when I am a part of it or I see my youth lead someone to Christ."
> - **Fruit of spiritual growth:** "Visible change and transformation of people's lives give me fuel for further work."
> - **Fruit of youth serving in ministry:** "I love to experience being used by God, and one of my biggest passions in ministry is seeing youth also experience being used by God"

Internal Fruit in Their Own Lives. While seeing fruit in those who they lead was highly motivating, recognizing fruit in their own lives was even more so to many of our motors. When reflecting on who they had become because of their involvment in ministry, they described a deepening faith, an intimacy with God, and an increasing love and compassion for youth. Often, this appeared to be more important than whether or not they saw visible fruit in the lives of youth. In fact, even though some of them were discouraged when talking about their ministry, they were full of excitement when talking about fruit in their personal lives as a result of their involvment in ministry. One motor described, "Before I began serving in ministry I was a good Christian who made good Christian decisions. Now, because of my involvement in ministry, my relationship with God has changed. Now, it's a constant and everyday relationship. It's a real and present friendship, not like a king-servant relationship." When asked what makes them effective in ministry, these motors described a deep dependence on

God, that they see fruit when they are in an intimate relationship with Jesus.

Many identified a direct connection between their fruitfulness and their commitment to the spiritual disciplines of prayer and fasting. In many ways these motors are living out the truths Jesus taught in John 15, "I am the vine; you are the branches. If you remain in me and I in you, you will bear much fruit; apart from me you can do nothing...This is to my Father's glory, that you bear much fruit, showing yourselves to be my disciples."

Meaning and Implications for Ministry
Fruit Inspectors

Fruitfulness in ministry is immeasurably important to people on the road to becoming motors in youth ministry. Often though, they are blind to the fruit that exists. They can be so self-critical that they don't see the fruit that is actually there. Regardless of where they are on the road to becoming a motor, whether at the very beginning or after a decade of ministry, motors sometimes need others to help them see the fruit in their ministries and their own lives.

Unfortunately, many motors described receiving quite the opposite from others. Instead of having someone support them, encourage them and inspire them to persevere in ministry, they often encountered cynicism and pessimism. One motor told of a time when he wanted to do something new in ministry and "an older person came up to me and said, 'Calm down! In time you'll see that it's not so easy. Don't worry, this enthusiasm will pass.'" Through our words and actions, we must instill faith and courage in these young motors, just as the Lord did with Joshua when He said, "Be strong and courageous. Do not be terrified do not be discouraged, for the LORD your God will be with you wherever you go." As Paul encouraged a young motor named Timothy, we can also encourage these motors, "Don't let anyone look down on you because you are young, but set an example for the believers in speech, in conduct, in love, in faith and in purity" (I Timothy 4:12).

We can play at least two important roles as spiritual "fruit inspectors." First, we can help them identify fruit in their lives and their ministries. Consider what prevents us from approaching a young motor and telling him or her that they are fruitful. Do we fear he or she will grow proud? Is the obstacle our own deficit mentaility? Is it a mistrust of compliments, encouragement and affirmation stemming from our historical and cultural roots? There may be many things which hold us back, but all motors need affirmation and encouragement. The ancient and powerful biblical concept of "blessing" needs to be revisited and reapplied in the context of our modern culture as we seek to be God's "voice" into the lives of young motors.

Our second role should be helping motors biblically define fruit in ministry. If we are to help them see and measure fruit, and applaud them for their faithfulness in serving the Lord, then we also need to help them know and articulate what good fruit is. The world around them is teaching this generation to be very pragmatic. Young motors need to understand the dangers of extreme pragmatism. If there is no visible fruit (increase in numbers of participants, for example), should they stop doing what they are doing? What do I do when I don't see fruit in my ministry? Is there fruit in ministry that is not visible? How much time do I need to persevere before I see the fruit I long for? Wise shepherds and mentors should help young motors wrestle through these questions as well as the discouragement that often comes when they do not see fruit. They need someone who will walk through those ministry valleys with them, seeking God together. Without a mentor or shepherd deeply and regularly involved in their lives, these motors may not see the fruit and draw the encouragement from God that they need to persevere in the difficult times in ministry.

Progress and quality are high values of this generation. They are highly motivating by a desire to develop innovative and effective methods and forms of ministry. This generation of motors has incredible potential. They are optimistic, creative, innovative, idealistic, and have tremendous vision for ministry, but they need us to come alongside and refuel them by helping them identify the fruit God is producing in their lives and the lives of others.

Finding 4
Growing Identity as a Motor

Not all motors are leaders, and not all leaders are motors. We were surprised to find that a few people we interviewed who had a leadership role and the appearance of success in ministry were not actually the motors they appeared to be. It was often hard to discern if someone was not a motor after all, or if they just had undeveloped potential or were at the beginning stages of their journey to becoming a motor. However, those who were further along on the road to becoming a motor in youth ministry shed light on how the process looked for them, and we discovered a common trait among them. Motors are in ministry because it is an expression of who they are, of their identity, not because it is a job to be done. More mature motors described a process of ever-increasing self-awareness about their identity as a person of influence. One motor summarized it very well. "It was a long process for me to realize I'm a leader. But over time it became more about who I was than what I was doing."

What did we learn about this growing self-awareness and acceptance of their identity as a leader or motor? We learned that each person had unique mile markers, events and rites of passage. But we also recognized some common themes which are worth paying attention to.

Awareness of a Need

Their growing understanding of identity as a person of influence often began with an awareness of need. Whether it was the lack of a youth leader, the need to help hurting teens, or the need to reach the lost with the gospel, motors were confronted with a need and someone challenged them to address that need.

Development of Knowledge, Skills & Heart

At the beginning of their involvement in ministry, motors described a time of developing the knowledge (head), skills (hands) and character and passion (heart) needed to be effective in ministry. The deeper they got involved in ministry, the deeper they experienced a "heart awakening" to the ministry. Their love and compassion grew deeper and deeper for the youth they served.

Aha! Moment: Shift from Doing to Being

Motors point to a critical moment—an event, conversation or experience—when they realized that they were a person of influence. This was the key shift, where ministry stopped being something they did, and became about living out their identity, serving out of an awareness of who they are and how they were created. Many motors in describing this moment said in essence, "That was when I accepted the fact that I am a leader."

One motor summarized his process in this way: "At first I didn't know I was a leader, but others thought I was. Then, I formally became the youth leader, but I didn't feel like their leader. Next I felt like a leader, but still had problems leading. Next I felt like a leader, their leader, and had no problem being with the group. Now I feel like a leader, feel good being with youth, and now want to become a leader of other leaders." In his experience, we see this progressive, growing self-awareness and acceptance of his identity as a leader, as well as the increasing confidence in his ability to lead.

Anointing and Commissioning

There was one other element that removed obstacles and helped them accept their identity: confirmation or anointing. At this point on the road to becoming a motor, they were all convinced that God wanted them to serve in this capacity. Yet they still needed confirmation of their influence both from those in leadership over them (pastor or priest), and from those they were leading (youth). This confirmation had a bigger impact on how they perceived themselves than how others perceived them, especially when it came from a pastor or priest. This sort of "anointing" not only enabled them to accept their leadership, but empowered them to lead courageously. The truth is, only a handful described experiencing this kind of anointing, but many more said they were craving it from their leadership.

Meaning and Implications for Ministry

As we develop leaders, we have to be aware that they will be full of self-doubt and need to have nurture and care. Motors in this generation need to know, as one motor put it, that „I am more important to you than what I do in ministry." Developing motors requires that we invest our time in shepherding, nurturing, encouraging, caring and mentoring them.

Some people can be described as "natural born leaders." Among the motors in youth ministry which we interviewed, there were a couple "natural born motors." But the overwhelming majority of motors were not born motors; they were formed into motors.

One of the most significant implications of this finding is that this growing self-awareness as a motor is a process of formation. It doesn't come automatically when authority, position or a title is bestowed on them.

We who are involved in church leadership often choose or appoint young leaders in a reactionary way instead of cultivating them. For example, there is a role that needs to be filled, and so we invite a 20-year-old to be the leader and then expect him or her to lead the whole ministry (often with very little support). We expect this person to have the skill and wisdom of a 40 year-old who has 20 years of ministry experience. We often act like we have the idea that when God calls someone, He will prepare them from A to Z. Then we'll have a leader ready to serve. All we have to do is just plug them in. We are reminded once again that this is a process. Motors need time, space, support, and the right environment to grow into the leaders the church needs.

In any professional sports team there are natural superstars. But the majority of the talented athletes are identified early as people with potential, then groomed and developed to become professional-caliber athletes. Similarly, in raising up leaders of the future, we in the church and other ministries in Poland must be willing to commit the time and energy required to identify and cultivate young motors to be the present and future leaders of God's kingdom work.

Finding 5
Need for a Mentor

One of the clearest findings of our study was the almost total lack of mentors involved in the lives of the young motors. Nearly all of those we talked to described having an example that they could follow, but not a mentor who invested in them. In fact, most described feeling ignored, overlooked and alone, or at worst, looked down upon and opposed by those over them. Motors pointed to three ways this lack of mentoring impacts them. First, it impacts their personal development as a leader. One girl said she could develop more as a leader if she had "an adult or pastor who would pray for me, be open to my ideas and help me with problems with people in the youth group." Second, it impacts their longevity in ministry. One motor explicitly stated that she fears she will eventually stop serving or quit growing because she lacks a mentor. Third, it impacts the fruitfulness of their work. One motor said, "Being left all alone, without support, puts the brakes on my ability to work effectively in ministry." On the road to becoming a motor in youth ministry in Poland, the lack of mentors is the "brake" which prevents them from accelerating forward in their development.

The truth is that there are so few motors in our study who said they have a mentor that we don't have enough data to compare motors with mentors to those without. Those who had a mentor were offered the mentoring relationship by the mentor. They were not the ones who sought out a mentor; the mentor sought them out.

The rare motors who had a mentor could not overstate how important this relationship was to them. But even more revealing, those who did not have a mentor were vocal about this topic. Without prompting, time and time again, they spoke of their longing to have a mentor who will invest in them personally and support them as they travel down the road to becoming a more effective motor in youth ministry. While they frequently listed the lack of a mentor as one of their greatest deficits and most important needs in ministry, they didn't assign blame or explain why they think this urgent need has gone unmet. The most striking thing was that the tone and emotion with which they spoke was not of anger or bitterness, but rather sadness and a sense of unfulfilled longing.

So what are they longing for, and what kind of mentor are they seeking? Motors spoke in one voice about the desire for relationship, not training or education. Relationship is one of the highest values of this young generation. They don't want information and teaching about ministry, but rather a relationship in which they can see and observe how what is taught is lived in the life of the mentor. In describing their image of a mentoring relationship, they used vivid, rich words such as an "older friend" or a "spiritual parent." These rich images reveal the longing of their hearts and should inform what the role of a mentor should be.

What qualities would they value in a mentor? These are some of the words they used to describe the kind of person whom they would trust: loving, authentic, vulnerable, open, transparent, real, and encouraging. They desire to be in relationship with mentor who will let them into the "inside" of the mentor's life. They need someone who will encourage them and believe in them, care for them and support them emotionally both in their personal life and ministry, listen and advise them about personal and ministry challenges, be a covering and protection for them, and help them with vision and direction in ministry.

Motors emphasized one other critical aspect of this mentoring relationship. They said, "We need mentors who will encourage us to action, stand next to us, help us with our problems, but not lead or take over the movement from us." For these motors, the ministry of mentoring is most of all a ministry of empowerment.

These motors are so hungry for mentoring that at the end of numerous interviews motors with deep gratitude thanked the interviewer and said that our initiation and pursuit of them as well as taking the time to ask questions and listen to them touched on their deep need for mentoring. One motor said to one of our interviewers, "The simple fact that you called me, as an older person...that you called me and think I have something to offer is very building and encouraging for me."

Meaning and Implications for Ministry

There are many definitions of mentoring, but one definition which closely matches what motors are longing for come from Eric Parsloe of The Oxford School of Coaching and Mentoring. He defines mentoring this way: "Mentoring is to support and encourage people to manage their own learning in order that they may maximize their potential, develop their skills, improve their performance and become the person they want to be." This definition touches on the areas of knowing, doing and being, and emphasizes the power of relationship.

It seems that for motors in this young generation, mentoring is an extension of a one-on-one, life-on-life discipleship relationship, but is also something more, or maybe the next step of discipleship, which touches not only their spiritual development but also their development in leadership. One of the challenges may be with the conflicting definition and expectations between the older and younger generations. The ideas of discipleship and mentoring are often associated with teaching or passing along information. This young generation longs for relationship and transformation. The differences in understanding the nature of mentoring and differences in expectations of the role of a mentor may be the greatest barrier preventing the older and younger generations from engaging in mentoring relationships.

Many of our motors indicated that because they have never been mentored, they often feel incapable of passing on the baton of leadership to the next generation. Could this also be one of the explanations for the lack of mentoring of this generation?

Whatever the causes of the current reality, there is no doubt that motors are crying out for mentors, older friends and spiritual parents who will pour themselves into these young leaders. This is an urgent challenge. As one motor put it, "Soon, today's 15 year-olds will be leading the church."

This brings us to some practical implications. First, churches and ministries need tools to call and equip mentors for these young motors. The role of training organizations such as Fala can be not only to serve churches through mentoring youth leaders, but also to provide tools and training for mentors.

Another implication for any church or organization who wants to train leaders is to evaluate the form of training in light of the need for mentoring. Mentoring does not always need to be long-term. It can be incorporated into each program in which motors, no matter what the age, are being challenged and equipped for ministry.

One last practical application is that mentoring can begin earlier than many would expect. Motors seemed to start searching for a mentor when they came to the point that they realized they couldn't do it alone. That means that teenagers who are beginning to serve while in junior high are already in need of a mentor. One striking insight is that many motors began to discover their passion for ministry at an early age. At this point, when someone begins to take their first steps in ministry, it is already appropriate for someone to come alongside them as a mentor.

We need to hear the heart of this generation, longing for spiritual leaders to pour into them so they can develop and be effective in their calling. A motor who was not part of this study recently wrote to a worker in Fala: "For a long time I've been praying for a mentor. In the past I've never had someone I could meet with regularly. However, I know that I need someone I can be accountable to, who would challenge me, encourage me, etc. In all this, I need someone who is also experienced in ministry. So I'm writing to you, because I'm unable to identify anyone from all the people I know who could be that kind of mentor for me. It's not that I have unreasonably high expectations. I am just looking for someone who has some kind of experience in this area."

DEEP DIVE

Finding 6
Shared Community-Based Ministry

Changes in the Youth Ministry Landscape

For years, the typical youth ministry in the local church in Poland had a leader who was appointed or elected. Most often they carried the burden of responsibility to organize the ministry activities and meetings alone. Through listening to motors, we see that ministry isolation has many contributing factors.

First, this style of leadership is often modeled in the church, and youth leaders simply imitate and reproduce what they have seen. Second, the Polish cultural value of a strong work ethic also contributes to this top-down leadership style. One motor who struggles with this "do-everything-myself mentality" confessed with a sense of guilt and confusion, "How can I ask someone else to do my job?" Third, motors said there is a mentality that only truly "spiritual people" are qualified to do ministry. Fourth, motors are easily discouraged when they encounter the false belief that youth aren't capable of doing anything significant. Youth themselves have believed this, and therefore often won't engage in serving alongside their leader. Then, the motor is left doing ministry alone. However, it is most discouraging when this message comes from the older generation. One motor said, "People in our age group are passionate about God and are ready to sacrifice for God. But churches don't respect or value young people. They want youth to be there, but don't think they have much to offer." Another motor currently in seminary said, "The church sometimes doesn't give a place for youth; it doesn't think young people are worth focusing on. Churches must understand young people and compromise in order to make it easier for youth to be involved. Church is for youth, the youth are not for the church."

As youth ministry developed in Poland, many youth leaders

began to build a volunteer staff or ministry team, primarily consisting of key youth involved in the ministry. Where these ministry teams existed, the leadership was still a top-down leadership style with the leader at the top leading his or her team. At least he or she wasn't alone anymore and had a team to work with, creating more fruitful ministry. While this team leadership is not everywhere, ministries in which a leader has a team seem to be healthier and have healthier leaders.

Paradigm Shift toward Community

As we talked to motors, we observed a paradigm shift which is beginning to happen in youth ministry in Poland. It is a bit paradoxical. Motors consistently expressed concern that this generation of young people is becoming more and more socially isolated and relationships more shallow because of the influence of social media. At the same time there is a shift toward leadership which functions in community and as community. Increasingly more ministries are being led by a group of peers, rather than by one youth leader who recruits a team. Even when there is a traditional youth leader, the way he or she relates to the ministry team is based less on authority or position and more on friendship.

The second critical aspect to this paradigm shift is that the motors of today's generation want to do something inter-denominationally and ecumenically. Even 10 years ago, youth ministry was primarily driven and organized by church denomination (Catholic, Baptist, Pentecostal etc.). Each denomination had its own conferences, camps etc. This is changing. Today's motors value their local churches, but simultaneously think outside of or beyond their own church and denomination. They are looking for unity within the universal church. They are tired of seeing divisions about differences and labels which aren't that important or relevant to them. Community, friendship, and unity are higher values to them than many of the doctrinal differences or historical conflicts which have divided the church. They are kingdom-oriented and want to unite to do something big for God.

Increasingly more organic and grass-roots movements are popping up in which youth cooperate and unite across denominational lines. These movements and ministries are interdenominational. They are characterized by a decentralized leadership, not based on the authority of one main leader but rather friendship, prayer and a common purpose. As one motor described the city-wide ministry, "We're just a bunch of friends from different churches who wanted to do something together for God." When these "groups of friends" work together in leadership, each person has a sense of ownership over the vision, direction, decisions and responsibilities. This leads to a different way of functioning and making decisions. One motor spoke of a New Year's conference that a group of friends organized, "It was more of a movement than something organized by an organization. Decisions were made differently than anything I had ever been a part of organizing before. There was friendship, trust and unity in our planning, organization and decision-making. And the whole event was covered in prayer by those of us organizing it. Every day, for eight hours a day in hour-long blocks of time and for two weeks before the event, there was one of us praying."

While these movements are led by a group or community of friends, they are not at all resistant to leadership and guidance. To the contrary, they deeply desire the support, mentoring, guidance, and encouragement of the older generation. One motor said, "We need more leaders who have a heart for youth and will come along side of us and help us accomplish our vision without taking control of the ministry." However, if this support is not provided, it appears they are motivated to reach their generation and will do it alone if they must.

DEEP
DIVE
52

Meaning and Implications for Ministry

In our training of leaders both nationally and in the local church context, there has long been the assumption that if we train and equip a leader, we will multiply the impact on the development of youth ministry in Poland. For years, Fala has offered conferences, training schools, and such to train the leader of a youth ministry, who in turn would lead his or her ministry more effectively. This paradigm shift toward groups of friends organizing organically and inter-denominationally has huge implications for our training ministry in Poland. We need new wineskins for the coming years of training and support.

One of the implications is that our training must have three critical elements: (a) life-on-life mentoring, (b) within the context of community, and (c) taking place in a live ministry setting. Training schools and conferences will continue to have their place and serve a purpose, but the old model of the experienced practitioner imparting knowledge and wisdom to the pupil through a conference will no longer be sufficient. New models of training are necessary. We need not only to meet the motors' needs and desires, but also to align ourselves to the ways Jesus trained and equipped his disciples in ministry through life-on-life relationships, in community, and on mission.

If our training needs to change, the ways we support motors in ministry must also be adjusted. Rather than always providing ready-to-use resources, we should provoke young motors to create new resources, programs, and ministries. The ways we create and distribute ministry resources must reflect this new paradigm of community. While there will remain a place for preparing and providing motors with resources for ministry, a new methodology should be employed in which Fala serves to empower motors to create for themselves new tools, resources and models of ministry within community, and then help them distribute those also through community.

Another practical role we can play is to create platforms where motors who are innovating new ministry models can come together and self-coach. Through our research and interviews with motors from all over Poland, we see that there are many small, grassroots movements in many different cities and regions. However, no one is bringing them together so that their innovative ideas can be multiplied and reproduced. In these situations, it is the young generation which owns the ministries. We can serve as connectors and catalysts by helping the movement multiply. One thing is clear: motors are not asking us to organize more conferences and trainings, but rather to give them the steering wheel and journey with them as they drive youth ministry forward into the future.

JV SLOVAKIA

What is the nature of emerging generation in Slovakia?

Maruška Kožlejová, Zuzana Potocká, Peter Michalčík, Darina Malá, Josh Howard, Ed Rumbold, Eva Kohútová, Marián Cabadaj, Peter Hrubo, Drahoslav Poloha, Ján Šimočko, Mark Chase, Zac Shepperson, Mike Sullivan, Anna Bakalárová, Katarína Leláková

Training Center Kompas (TCK) was founded in 1993 when leaders from different churches throughout Slovakia initiated a network of youth ministries and organizations called SIE (Network). From the start, TCK has had a clear vision to help the generation of Christ´s followers appearing after the fall of Communism. Over time, Kompas has become a training center with the goal of encouraging youth ministry in local churches.

In recent years Kompas has expanded its training space to include many different activities and projects. Some of these are oriented toward sharing the gospel (for example, English Conversational Camps, preventive antidrug program, EXIT tour, and Fusion, which is a music project in the community). Others focus on discipleship (for example, the School of Leaders and Youth Leaders Conference).

Our vision is to be part of a movement of God among the youth of Slovakia that finds its home in the local church and transforms society. Our purpose is to train, help, and inspire youth leaders who are raising up the next generation of Christ followers in the church. Our core values are Dependance upon God, God Honoring Excellence, Love communicated through grace and truth, Personal growth, Faithfulness, and Deep integrity.

We currently minister in five locations around Slovakia: Bratislava, Banská Bystrica, Prešov, Levice, and Žilina. Our workers are involved in local church youth ministries in each of these locations. Our desire is to offer inspiration, training, and examples for youth ministries. Therefore, the question we chose for this research was the following:

What is the nature of the emerging generation in Slovakia?

A team of fifteen Kompas staff members comprising of twelve Slovaks and three Americans designed and executed this Deep Dive research project. We focused on youth from 14 to 16 years of age. We realized that since these youth will one day be youth leaders in this country, it is important to fully understand them. We convened one-on-one, in-depth interviews with 120 youth from across the country. The sample was equally distributed among boys and girls, between those who live in the villages, towns and cities, from gymnasium (higher competency) and other high schools (lower competency), and church and unchurched youth.

We wanted to learn how we can make our ministry increasingly more relevant for today´s Slovak youth. Slovakia, as well as the rest of Central and Eastern Europe, has undergone great changes in recent years, not only in political systems, but also in this generation's sociological, anthropological, and philosophical perceptions and understandings the world. This project was designed to help us explore the nature and needs of the emerging generation of youth.

A post, post-communistic Generation

We can no longer call the present generation of youth post-communistic. Their perception of the world and problems are no longer directly affected by communism or socialism. It is now highly influenced by a desire for material security, free choice, and free speech. The generation of youth we used to work with after the fall of Communism was characterized by a certain depth of character because their thinking was shaped by a thirst for freedom. Their concerns were similar to the concerns of their parents. Their possibilities were limited by lack of opportunities and freedom not only in the area of job success, but also in critical thinking, faith, and intellectual discoveries and breakthroughs.

After the time since the fall of communism, we began to see noticeable differences in the behavior and thinking of the youth. For example, in one of our English camps, we used to do "culture talks" – themes about cultural differences. In these talks we warned American students who came to teach English language not to be discouraged in situations where they would ask a question and the Slovak students would be silent and look at ground, even when they knew the answer. During communism, the safest way to behave was not to attract attention to yourself or stand out in the crowd. If you did, it was very easy for you to become an unwanted person as much as a class enemy. We would tell the Americans that if a Slovak student gave the right answer, their friends would consider it showing off or boasting. The Post-communistic young generation, who we used to work with, was characterized by a certain degree of reticence and humbleness.

The data from this research supports much of what we have been teaching about cultural differences. However, we are seeing some significant differences. The emerging generation is a capitalistic generation, along with everything that a capitalistic orienta-

DEEP DIVE

tion implies: freedom of thinking, expression, travel, and the desire and expectation of material and financial safety. It is the generation which is not afraid to ask questions, doubt authorities, and discover new opportunities. This young generation is often encouraged to have high ambitions by their parents and grandparents, who sometimes even uncritically urge them to make their dreams come true through things that they, because of the political system in which they were raised, did not have and were not able to seek.

The generation of parents are shifting to a dangerous pole of unprecedented and above-standard material safety. They are doing everything possible to ensure their children enjoy comfort and choice. They provide them with the ability to travel and live a quality life, even at the cost of their own absence in their children´s lives due to work. That´s what we learned in many interviews. And so, although this generation does not lack the finances to improve their lives, they desperately miss attention, authority, and friendship. A big theme which arises for them is love, in both directions, and how they accept love, when they feel they are love, and when they give love.

Before we explore the theme of love, let's discuss one other phenomenon. Among students who we were interviewed, we discovered certain differences not only in the answers, but also in their over-arching approach to life. This phenomenon is so significant that we want to describe it in order to better understand other findings. We found students to belong to one of two groups: the overly busy group and the bored group.

Finding 1
Two Extremes

While doing the interviews, we discovered two very strong categories of students, and two very opposite groups: the overly busy group of students, and the bored group of students.

The overly busy group of students

These students have a lot of activities outside of school – athletic practices, drama schools, music lessons, and language schools. They say that a significant part of their friends have a very similar life as well. They do not have any free-time to relax. They feel pressured by parents to accomplish a lot and achieve great results in everything. It appears that parents often are fulfilling their own dreams through their children. (We surmise that they want to make up for fact that they didn't have chance to study the languages they wanted, couldn't travel, and were very limited during communism and the years immediately following). They push their children to have a better life than they have had.

Youth leaders, as well as our future youth leaders are growing out of this group of students. Because they have abilities and talents, they will be most likely be chosen for leadership roles in churches and youth groups. We can meet people like this in our training projects such as The School of Leaders and Conference for Youth Leaders. We have already experienced some tension with attendance and conflict of priorities when we invite young people to School of Leaders and our school and church events. (Interestingly, we also observed that most students from this group have complete family units.)

The bored group of students

This bored group is in many ways the opposite. When these

students describe their typical day, they speak of it as a never-ending boredom that starts at school and continues as they come home. They are on Facebook excessively and are going out with the same group of people with whom they are bored. They lack ambition and a clear purpose in life. They are passive and apathetic. They want holiday to be over after two weeks because it is less boring when they are in school. It is hard for them to think about the future. They don't have a clear idea of what they want to do.

We need to reach these students too. We need youth from this second group in our evangelism projects like FUSION, KECY and EXIT. (We took note that more of this second group of students came from incomplete families, most missing fathers.)

Application for our ministry

If this is so, can our training programs (School of Leaders, conferences, etc.) help to bring balance to lives of busy students as well as motivation and engagement to those who are bored?

Finding 2
Love: recieving love and feeling loved

Description

As we explored the nature of the emerging generation, we found a strong need for love. Students spoke of this many times and in many ways. This aspect of their experience included, but is not limited to, the following: spending time with others, the need of being included, and desire to belong somewhere. When we talked to them about things like respect, friendship, and family (present or future), they spoke of their need for love. Their response to the question, When do you feel that someone loves you? is similar to one 14 year-old who said, "[I am loved] when they stop by and talk to me …when they invite me out." And in the words of a 16 year-old girs, we heard the answer, "When they care...about me."

There was one central theme threading through all of their statements. People in this age group have difficulties understanding love as an abstract notion. They need to see an act or deed. A specific manifestation of interest is a signal that someone cares about them and loves them. We also learned that as in other areas, such as respect and justice, their thinking exhibits a minimalizing of the idea of love. It's as if they don't consider themselves worthy enough to be fully loved, so they reduce love to the idea of being included. To them, love equals belonging, and belonging means inclusion. We found that even despite the realization of injustice in the world and incomplete relationships within the family, students expressed that they dream about love, a good life, and having a good husband or wife. They seemed to desire love but saw it as something they couldn't affect, as if it would simply be there or not. They didn't see it as depending on their decisions.

Application for our ministry

If this age group conncects love to a specific action or deed, then it's important that our activities (and especially our followup) are focused on involving students in the activity itself. We have to find ways students can be a part of the process of program design so that they can experience the act of inclusion and find their place. We need to challenge their idea that just being included means the same thing as being loved as well. We need to lead them to a deeper understanding of love. We can learn a lot from our project Fusion. The ministry is based on the experience of being in a loving community, of belonging, and of belonging to something bigger than themselves. We could apply this strategy to our other projects such as EXIT or English Camps.

Finding 3
Love: giving love and value in helping

Description

It was surprising to find that teenagers wanted people to say good about them:

> I want other people to say about me, after I die, that in some way I helped them, even though it was a small thing... That I was willing to help them when they had some problems.

When they thought about their future, and what mattered to them when they imagined being 30-40 years old, were things like a good family, good job, a car, and a place to live. However, when we asked them what they want people to say about them after they die, their answers sounded like this: "That I was there for them. I was there to help them anytime." No car, no family, and no job were mentioned.

These two responses appear to line up. How? What are the reasons for that? Our suggestion is that it has a lot to do with immediate self-gratification. While still alive, they want to be happy and have things. They know that when they die, they cannot take the stuff with them and it doesn't matter anymore. However, the idea that someone will miss them because they were helpful and needed gives them a feeling of gratification right now even as they are thinking about it. It is important to note here, that they not only want to help others, but they also expect that their effort will be appreciated while they are still alive.

There are three important implications for us in this:

1. It says a lot about how they **see their own value**. They need to be needed. They want to have a special place in people's lives. They may even want to be irreplaceable

(i.e., they want others to miss them). In some way, by putting themselves in important places in other people's lives, they may even get into a position to receive someone's love.

2. For them, to help means **to love**. When they are not able to help someone, they are sad. It hurts them to see their loved ones in need. Help may be a genuine expression of love, as well as a channel through which we can communicate to them our love.

3. Being able to help gives them **hope**. When they can help someone, it may mean several things: (a) they demonstrate good character; (b) they are more skilled in certain areas than other people; and (c) they have resources to help. This gives them hope that they are "someone," that they have value.

Our findings in this area definitely counter the assumption that teenagers are nothing but selfish and self-centered. Also, they show us the folly of assuming that when young people express a longing to be needed and important, they just want to use that as a means to get something for their own use. Of course, there is a certain degree of selfishness in this, as there is with all sinful people. And of course, there is this issue of gratifying one's own desires. But in helping another they accomplish at least three things: (a) they really help someone; (b) they satisfy their need to be needed; (c) they will see themselves as more valuable when people appreciate their effort.

Application for our ministry

How can we then help them? We need to balance all these areas. It would be dangerous to create cheap and superficial opportunities for them to help, and thus give them false impressions, false hopes, or make them addicted to the idea that "if I am needed, then it will make me feel so good."

How can we create a space and opportunity for them to help? How can we better communicate to them that we love them by helping them? How can we help them to help others by using their own talents, gifting, etc.? This would be a huge opportunity to help them (a) find passion in their lives, (b) develop personally, and (c) live more like Jesus – helping humbly and not for cheap fame.

Finding 4
Generation of "here and now"

Description

Another significant characteristic we learned about this emerging generation is that they exist in a fast, dynamic, and virtual reality. The catalyst for this appears to be the internet, social networks, and smartphones that allow them to have acces to everything everywhere. They spend enormous amounts of time on internet. Parents have no possibility to check or have control over what they are doing and visiting online. Because of smartphones, they are not in the living room or on the family computer where parents can see what they are watching. It has become a personal and secret platform for living. They try to find help online and seek information of all kinds that they need. Since they have access to so much, they feel like they have been everywhere and seen everything despite the fact that they have never left their hometowns. They spend most of their time on Facebook, sharing and following their friend's online existence, their statuses, comments, photos and videos.

In social networking there is opportunity for a kind of self-expression young people don't have in the real life. They feel free.

They express how they feel, what pleases them, what they are upset about, where they are going, what they plan to do, and what they dream about. The virtual world gives them possibility of free emotional expression.

Everything in the lives of these young people happens fast. The daily activities of all their friends are accessable on Facebook and so if they miss something, they feel like a failure. This is also the chance for young people who are not sociable, to present themself any way they like. All activities online happen fast and change quickly. They trend one way on one day and then change the next day. They have to choose in a moment if they will be part of something online(trend, group, event). Their onlne existence defines them.

In real life there is no chance to maintain so many friendships, groups of people, meetings, conversations as they can on Facebook. They can be part of societies that are controversial or have no meeting points outside of the internet. They can choose how to present themselves. By choosing photos, videos, likes, and groups, they can paint the picture of who they are. Real life is reduced to virtual life. But for them it is real. Even on the virtual platform, they share real feelings.

Application for our ministry

If we want to be an influential part of the emerging generation and if we want to reach them, we have to get our projects and ourselves to where youth are, and that means virtual space. We cannot stay passive and static observers of online reality. We have to be proactive in our approach with news, invitations, reactions to their online lives. We need to engage them with discussions, questions, challenges and encouragments. We also have to find a way to connect them with reality again.

Another application for us is to understand that in the past we needed to build relationships with people years before we shared gospel. But this generation is living in the here and now. They are ready to listen here and now. They live in this moment, and so we should spread the gospel more openly and freely because their openess to gospel is greater than in the previous generation.

Finding 5
Changed paradigm of authorities

Description

Connection and contact with friends is very important for this generation. It's even a must. On one hand, it is natural for youth of this age. On the other, the authority that once belonged to parents and teachers (as a traditional authority for development of opinions) is now occupied by a group of friends to whom they belong. If a person's ability to accept another unconditionally is this generation's highest test of character, then parents and other traditional authority figures are in trouble. Potentially, parenting is in a crisis because of this conflict of authority. It creates disconnection with parents. This can lead to a desperate condition of loneliness if their friends leave or reject them, because parents are no longer the foundational relationship on which to fall back.

There is a growing gap between youth and their parents. Youth are becoming more and more independent. Their autonomy is growing. At an increasingly younger age they have an opportunity to earn money at part time jobs, eat in fast food restaurants or order their food online. They can communicate with anybody in the world, even in other languages, and usually better than their parents. They have better control over their life than the generations before them.

There are dealing with divorces, incomplete families, and parents who have to work abroad for better pay, which exacerbates the disconnection. Many students admit that their parents are going through a divorce, and this is causing them to feel confused, angry, and guilty. When we asked them about how they are spending a normal day, very few mentioned time with their parents. When we were interpreting the data from the interviews, we saw that young people are materially supported, but they lack the time and undivided attention of their parents.

The question for us is how Kompas can help in this situation, when our main focus is not the family. This vacuum and absence of parental authority notably affects our ministry. This information is markedly important for the Christian communities, which should strategically engage parents even in serving youth. We should help young people spend more time with their parents. And we should create a picture and example of how a biblical family should look for kids with incomplete families.

Finding 6
Dreams

Description

It is commonly assumed that teenagers always dream, and have naive, unrealistic dreams. The truth is that for many of them this is not true:

> Dreams? I don't have them yet. I hope I will reach my goals. But I don't know yet what I want....

> Dreams? I don't know... It's not that I don't have them, they're simply not anything special.

Why is this so? What are the causes?

DEEP DIVE

They seem to need dreams that can provide quick gratification, so they end up with a dream for today. Or even more precisely, they follow their minimalistic definition of a dream: "Do what you like." This isn't a bad definition. The problem lies in taking and liking things without sorting them out, without judging whether they are worth trying, or whether they are worth investing in. Rather than pursuing some future dreams, they take into their hands what is immediately at their disposal, and those are often cheap dreams. Is it laziness? Pessimism? Certainly, it is a form of minimalizing: "I take what satisfied me right now."

They probably don't even know how to develop a dream. And even if there is a dream starting to appear, they do not know how to pursue their dreams. They are not active. Why? They don't see immediate results. They don't get immediate satisfaction. They seem to have no motivation and perseverance to pursue their dreams. They think they still have time to figure it out, and that is acceptable to them. There seems to be an enchanted circle: "No dreams, no driving force. No driving force, no dreams." We need to break this somehow! (It would be interesting whether the pressure of having a dream increases when they get older and have to decide what they want to do with their lives.)

It is interesting how their "I want to travel" dreams fit into this. Many of them have dreams of traveling the world one day or at least traveling to many countries. They picture choosing the best one to settle in. How can we use this to help them pursue their dreams? Can we find some principle, some hidden secret in this? Why is travelling so attractive? Is it only because it helps them to escape the present reality? Or is it just a minimalistic solution (or escape) for not being deeply satisfied with their present life?

Another common thing is that they are afraid they will not reach their goals, they will not get to live their dreams, and they will end up disappointed.

Application for Ministry

It is interesting to see the differences between people who have and those who do not have dreams. Young people who have dreams for their future and who have "the fuel" to pursue them are usually those who have some hobbies, interests, role models, and people to encourage them to pursue their dreams. These people are usually more disciplined in how they spend their free time. Having no time is one obstacle hindering people from pursuing their dreams. We need to help them to see that it is necessary to make small steps and persevere even though we do not see immediate results. How can we achieve this? How can we provide positive and realistic encouragement as they start to develop and keep pursuing their dreams?

Finding 7
The Idea of a Successful Life

Description

During our interviews we asked students (14 to 16 years old) this question: How do you imagine a good, successful life? The answers of students led us to the conclusion that there are two groups of people, and their ideas are different. The first group of students values the quality of life and success. They relate to the "Hear and Now."

This group is made of students from less prestigious high schools and families. Their answers did not touch on the importance of studying, school results, or a choice of school when they thought about a successful life. The respondents connected a good life with the opportunity for travel, new experiences, the need to be here and now for somebody. Their ideal day does not have anything to do with school, education, or the future. The main image of good and successful looks like this: money and work, and in that order. For them, work should be amusing, with less work hours and mainly well paid. Good life also means spending enough time with friends. In some cases, the "here and right now" led to boredom and apathy in connection with their future.

The other group of students is characterized by valuing the quality of life, good life, success, and reaching certain goals in future. For this group, students have more ambitions; their answers were connected with education, but their thinking was minimalized here as well. They were still thinking "here and right now," but more specifically, "job and money." This group understands the connection between performance, achievement, and reward. This group has ambitions to earn a lot of money, without need to "count every cent." They explore and acknowledge themselves, not only spending time working, but also in having fun. Enough financial security is the integral part of life. Most of them mentioned, for example, "I surely should be able to live in a house."

This group of students has a tendency to learn and acknowledge themselves, including the spiritual world with an intellectual side. We can interest them by scholarly lectures, articles and facts, suitable to their age and open to intellect. This group needs activities with opportunity for personal growth and development of their competencies.

For both groups of students the successful life includes their feelings, pleasures, personal interests, travelling/exploring new places and cultures, and the use of modern technologies in connection with social life, specifically with network of acquaintances. Having enough financial resources is considered one of the key factors in the matter of good and successful life. They think, "I don't have to think if I can afford to buy things."

In the generation "here and now" we have noticed a sort of shadow of constant fear over their responses and their perception

of the world. When we looked for the reasons in the data of the interviews, we found that young people from ages 14-16 are
- afraid of bad results whether at school or in their personal efforts,
- afraid that whatever they are working on might go wrong,
- afraid of disappointing their close relatives or friends,
- afraid of spoiling the relationships in their families and losing or misunderstanding their friends,
- afraid of breaking families,
- afraid of loneliness,
- afraid of not being accepted,
- afraid of unfairness,
- afraid of bad decisions, and
- afraid of bad qualities of people.

Application for our ministry

We should be very careful working with the youth, so that they don't find themselves in positions where they are afraid. We have to be very sensitive and offer something different from their everyday environment, whether at school, at home or with their friends. While doing projects like EXIT, FUSION or KECY English ministry, we should encourage them a great deal and adopt a loving and accepting attitude. When students normally expect a standard reaction from us, we have to give them hope and explain and remind them how special they are.

Finding 8
Addictions and Idolatry

One young girl once defined her generation like this: "This young generation is a generation of idolaters." Satan came to Jesus and told Him: "The devil led him up to a high place and showed him in an instant all the kingdoms of the world. And he said to him, "I will give you all their authority and splendor; it has been given to me, and I can give it to anyone I want to," Luke 4: 5-6. This is exactly how young people think – they want authority and splendor, they want all the kingdoms of the world and want it everything immediately and without work. And the devil uses exactly this tool. They don´t have a problem to bow to that.

These are the kinds of things we heard from these students:

> I would never go on a potato picking like my mom went. But we are all like that, we want everything to be given to us, we always choose the easier way to get what we want. My friends are totally crazy about games and the Internet. They spend hours there, and they don´t have control over it. (Boy, 16 years old)

> The most important thing is to be on Facebook, that´s where everything happens. This is where my real life exists. I hate my parents when they forbid me being there, so they forbid me to live. (Girl, 14 years old)

> Most of all I want to have a successful life. I would give everything so I could enjoy it and have enough money. (Boy, 16 years old)

We don´t think that Facebook itself is an idol; it is more like a platform where idolatry happens. If there was no Facebook, they would probably find another platform where idolatry could continue. We could call idols the following:

- ➢ Groups of friends, friendships, acceptance, the need to be connected and presented
- ➢ Computer games
- ➢ Successful life and money – they would give their soul to have their success quickly and free of charge

Finding 9
Minimalizing

Description

When we looked for themes more significant than others, we found out that this generation is a generation of minimalizing, but in a rather negative way. Their understanding of life is reductionist, from lasting, important, and precious values to something lesser which satiates them. In interviews with students we heard about the value placed in "respect and understanding." Students seemed to be united in their opinions regarding respect and toleration. Here are some of the answers to the question: Do you feel you are understood by your parents/adults?

I don´t think there´s anything about me, that people don´t understand. I am not sure if it is even possible to really understand somebody. (Boy, 16 years old)

My parents don´t have to understand me, I just want them to respect me. It is the same with my friends, some are like me, some are not, but I have to respect them all. (Girl, 15yrs)

You don´t need to understand your children; just let them do what they want. (Boy, 15yrs)

Students don't expect they'll be understood, in fact they presume they won't be. To be respected is rated higher than to be understood or understand the others. Young people desire freedom more than understanding by other people.

They talk a lot about respect. But what they mean by respect is tolerance. The idea of respect has been reduced or "minimalized" to acceptance without judgment. Even though our questions were orientated to the relationship between adult and student, we heard features about norms for relationship between peers and friends also. Throughout our interviews, the minimalistic nature of this generation became more and more obvious. Understanding is reduced to respect, which is then reduced to tolerance. This generation does not long to understand or to be understood, they only want to be tolerated. Young people have lower expectations regarding what they can get from life and the others.

Another example of minimalizing in this generation is its image of family. Youth do not expect support, protection, love or acceptance; it is enough for them that they actually have a family, even if it is not complete. **Real life is minimalized to virtual life. Fairness is minimalized to tolerance. Love is reduced to the fact that they belong somewhere and are accepted.**

Application for our ministry

If it is true, that this generation doesn´t desire understanding, only tolerance and the need to be heard, then we have to understand three things:

1. We should try to be open for young non-believers who want to share their thoughts and opinions with us. In our relationships, there ought to be some kind of tolerance combined with pieces of Biblical views about specific areas. Young people should experience the feeling of being graciously known.

2. Young Christians should be advised of the importance of understanding, not just tolerating someone. Luke 19:5 says, "When Jesus reached the spot, he looked up and said to him, "Zacchaeus, come down immediately. I must stay at your house today." Jesus craved knowing and understanding people. Because we are Christians, our mission is not to tolerate people, but to join in a relationship of understanding and real interest.

3. In our programs, we should point to the ways Jesus came to give us life and fulfillment so the complete gospel is not minimized or reduced, but it is a fullness of grace, love and understanding.

Program Experiments

While doing our research about the nature of the coming generation, we came to a conclusion that there are many aspects of our ministry that we need to redesign and improve. Data indicate that:

1. Young people are interested in spiritual things, but they do not have much time or relationship to be exposed to straight gospel. (It is a "here and now" generation.)

2. We need to work more in a virtual world, because that is the place where they are most of the time – starting with promotion, lectures and a demonstration of interest in their lives.

3. We need to shorten our speeches, lectures and topics almost to half time (mx. 15-20 min). As stimuli increase for these young people, they cannot concentrate on one input for a long time.

4. We need to change the paradigm of "theater" programs (wherein young people come and watch the prepared program) to a concept where they will be involved and needed, and where their gifts will be visible.

5. The desire to get some interest and to be heard in our ministry can be fullfilled by an emphasis on close and personal discipleship (life-to-life). We need to help our youth leaders understand this concept.

6. If we want to become natural authority in lives of these youth, we cannot be authoritarian. We have to gain authority naturally by becoming members of their groups or becoming their real friends.

An experiment we have decided to run in response to these findings is to change our paradigm of relating to parental authorities. This experment relates to the disconnection between youth and their families. We decided to do it at the English camp called KECY in Presov congregation of ELC in the beginning of July.

During the camp we first decided to observe the students and then to write a postcard to each parent. In those notes we will express our gratitude for allowing their children to come to our camp. We will also write about the special and good things we noticed about their child (for instance their care about the others, their athleticism, excellent English skills, their qualities such as: kindness and consideration, and so forth). We will send this postcard so that the parents will receive it before their child comes home. We will also invite them to the goodbye party with the Americans.

Last year we tried to invite parents to a goodbye party and only about four people out of 50 came. The first criterion of data from the experiment will be the number of parents at the party. (We see the merit in this because in the past some parents forbade many of their children to come to our church after the camp). They will be able to see how it works and meet the leaders who created the programs. Through it we will build trust.

The second aspect of the experiment, a bit harder to measure, is our desire to increase their interest in the ministry because of what they experience. We hope that when we tell the students about our plan, they will be prepared to be sent such a postcard, and they will also be able to communicate more openly.

Since the initial writing of this report, we have had the chance to run the experiment. Here are the results:

We had 18 parents coming to the goodbye party with American team. One third of the participant's parents joined us. Compare to last year, this is huge increase. Also we have heard from the students that parents were calling their children while they were still at camp, telling them about the invitation card sent by the first class. They seemed to appreciate our effort and decided to come to the party to meet the Slovak and American team.

We tried to spend some time with parents at the party and personally heard from two parents that they are really glad to meet people who influenced their children so much. We also talked to a mother of one of the students from last year's camp. Throughout the year she had a big problem with her daughter going to church to attend youth group. After meeting the team she said she finally understood and approved her daughter to continue coming. She said it was beautiful what we were doing and is glad that her daughter found such a good friends. Parents even enthusiastically joined the games. Our team leader expressed gratitude to the parents for entrusting us and sending us such a uniquely wonderful group of students to camp.

Overall, we felt like an experiment was successful. It produced a lot of good and healthy fruit and helped build relationships with parents, opening new ways of communication. We are recommending that all of our camps in other cities try this as well.

JV UKRAINE

DEEP DIVE

What is happening in the hearts of Ukrainian young people after English Camp?

Roman Dziubak, Roman Sandulskiy, Anatoliy Pishchaliuk, Justine Bosovych, Esty Kovalchuk, Marta Palamar, Tania Shkuratova, Natalia Shepeleva, Anna Stepanenko, Svitlana Shymkiv, Maryna Zhuk, Eduard Kurat, Elena Kurat, Christina Zborivska, Ruslan Stropysh, Sviatoslav Garvas, Yulia Sandulska, Olga Vozna, Yulia Zvizlo, Tomasz Chmiel, Alla Pishchaliuk, Dima Sokolov, Ben Williams, Kristy Williams

Josiah Venture has partnered with Ukrainian local churches to share the gospel with young people at English camps since 2004. Together, the Josiah Venture team and Ukrainian church leadership teams have focused on sharing the gospel clearly and in a contextually relevant way. The team has been pleased to see students at every camp respond to the gospel with repentance and faith. Also, the Josiah Venture team recognizes that repentance is just the first step on a journey to transform young people into disciples who make disciples. To do this, campers must become rooted in the local church. One of the largest problems in Ukraine is anchoring new believers in church communities. Our experience is that less than 50% of people who repent at camp are later involved in the local church.[2,3]

We have attempted to address this issue in the past by refining the gospel message to focus more on what "life in Christ" looks like after repentance. In addition we have discussed the costs of following Jesus. These changes help to clarify the gospel and reduce the number of people who claim they have repented. However these changes have not increase the percentage of youth who are connected to local church communities in the months following camp.

Josiah Venture Ukraine determined to explore the most pressing issue for our youth ministry context:

What is happening in the hearts of Ukrainian young people after English Camp?

The Deep Dive Ukraine team chose to focus on students who came to English camp in 2012 and 2013, and who, while there, had indicated that they had made a decision to follow Christ. A majority of the interviews were conducted with students who are neither connected to nor growing in the local church. This sample was chosen to better understand the hearts of these students in hopes of meeting their needs and helping them grow in Christ.

The Deep Dive team that conducted this study included 21 Ukrainians from six different churches in three different cities. Together, this team developed a protocol to better understand the hearts of these young people. The Deep Dive team met together in March of 2013. After the protocol was developed, the team conducted a total of 56 interviews from March through May of 2013.

To conduct an interview, an interviewer contacted a young person and invited him or her to a neutral meeting place. The

---
[2] Data was evaluated from 2011 and 2012 English Camps
[3] Repentance- is self-proclaimed. On the last day of camp, campers complete a survey and indicate if /how they have responded to the gospel

interviewer then assured the student that the purpose of the time was to better understand young people in Ukraine and evaluate Josiah Venture camps. Students were assured that their individual responses would remain anonymous. While conducting an interview, each interviewer captured data through hand-written notes. Interviewers were instructed to listen well and not to correct mistaken theology or the opinions of the interviewees. The Deep Dive team recognized that the time conducting the interviews was ministry in itself and provided great opportunities to deepen relationships with young people.

Finding 1
The Family

Description

One of the most common themes during interviews was regarding family. Ukrainian young people desire closer relationships with their immediate family members and especially with their parents. At the same time, most families are in disarray. One student said, "I would like for my relationship with my parents to be repaired." Ukrainian families are often marked by stories of alcoholism, parents working abroad, limited financial resources, absent fathers, and separated or divorced parents. Many young people indicated they wanted to be married later in life but did not want a marriage like their parents. Many female students indicated that their best friend is their mom. Nearly everyone stated that their parents have significant influence in their lives. Another student remarked, "I used to have a bad attitude towards my parents, and they also did towards me. But now I would like to change that." Another student said, "For me, my family's opinions are my primary concern."

Many parents are opposed to the Evangelical church, however.

Others are indifferent. Many parents from traditional (Greek Catholic, Ukrainian Orthodox) church backgrounds are antagonistic toward the Evangelical church, even if they themselves do not attend a traditional church.

Parents care greatly about the future of their sons and daughters and want them to be successful. The primary goals of parents for their children are health, good grades, admission into university, and finding a good job. These priorities are emphasized in such a way that other activities, which might distract youth from these primary goals, are discouraged. If young people desire to connect to a youth group or local church, there is often tension between them and their parents. Parents do not see the value of church and might even be opposed to this new "religion." This tension between church and family stems from a perception that the two are seemingly incompatible and require a choice – either belong to an Evangelical youth ministry or be in good graces with the family.

Meaning and Implications

Parental and familial support is essential in church efforts to make disciples of young people. When young people feel that they must choose between family and being a part of a local youth group, they will consistently choose family.

Without the support of their parents, there are significant challenges to long-term disciple-making relationships with these students. Despite broken families, young people care most about their parents' opinions. This challenges the assumption that young people are independent thinkers who primarily make their own decisions. Ukrainian young people want to please their parents. It is important for churches to develop relationships with these parents. Parents must see the value of youth ministry in the local church in order for young people to be consistently involved.

Since young people feel forced to choose between church and

family, we must find ways to come alongside families and not compete with them. The local church must make an effort to build relationships with parents and family both before and immediately after camp so that the important institutions of family and Christian community are not at odds. The church should think about ways to serve the family and meet the needs of parents. How can the church meet the physical, social, and spiritual needs of families? How can the church support the goals and desires that parents have for their children?

Finding 2
Friends

Description

Friends were the second most common theme emerging from the interviews with Ukrainian young people. Friends are considered an extension of family. Groups of friends are typically small and take years to develop and establish trust. Youth are completely open with their closest friends and share about the deepest problems in their lives. Friends are loyal; they stick together. Relationships with friends often fill the voids left by poor relationships in families. Friends have significant influence on one another and desire to inspire each other for the better. One student said, "I have the desire to change my character so that I can improve my relationships with my friends."

Often when new believers return home to their friends after camp, they do not know how to articulate what occurred there. They do not know how to share about their new relationship with God, and they do not know how to connect their friends and family to it. This unique experience at camp has created a gap between new believers and their friends. Over time, new believers sense that they need to make a decision between their old friends and new Christian friends. Many choose their long-time friends. Young people with few or no close friends before camp were more likely to get connected to the youth group.

Meaning and Implications

Friends play a significant role in the lives of Ukrainian young people. They are almost at the same significance level as family. Friends have significant influence over one another. Prior to this study we had not noticed that young people desire to influence each other in positive ways.

New believers face a choice between old and new friends after camp. Many youth workers encourage new believers to become a part of the youth group and join a new community of friends. However, these youth workers fail to realize that they are often challenging youth to leave their oldest and closest relationships.

In the past, we assumed that friends distract one another from hearing and responding to the gospel. For fear of disruption, we often intentionally divided groups of friends at camp. However, this study challenges that practice. Keeping friends together at camp will introduce the gospel to their friendship circles and likely be more fruitful long term.

The local church will need to pay special attention to groups of friends. The strategy to reach youth should include reaching whole groups of friends. Churches should target entire social groups or an entire class in schools. The local church must look outside of individual salvation and revisit a group approach to evangelism.

The local church must also equip new believers to become missionaries to their friends. Campers are more in tune with their friends and more aware of their spiritual needs, thus making them more effective to reach out to their circles of influence. Josiah Venture material like "LOOK" and "SHIFT" can help train new believers to be effective evangelists, even at a young age or while still young in the faith.

Finding 3
Future Disappointment

Description

During the interviews every young person spoke about the future. The ultimate goal for these young people was to be married and to have a family and a good job. The path to this future was typically understood to be one of diligent study in high school in order to pass entrance exams and attend an institution of higher education. Provided that students do well in university, they hope to get a good job upon graduation. They hope marriage and family naturally materialize along the way. The key milestones along this path are entrance exams, university acceptance, and securing a job. Young people and their parents feel a sense of urgency surrounding education and work. There seems to be no other path forward. Money and a more comfortable life are key goals.

However, the hope for a successful future is often overshadowed by the foreboding sense of impending disappointment in life. Their hope is quite delicate. They anticipate that there will be disappointment around every corner. Many of the students have experienced shattered dreams in their pasts. They dream of having a great marriage, but they have been disappointed by their parents' marriages. They dream of a having a good family but they do not want the relationships to be like those in their own families. One student said, "Because of the negative example of my parents and other close people, I have lost faith in marriage and family." Dreams of getting into college and getting a good job are shattered by a crooked educational system in Ukraine. Bribery and corruption infiltrate all aspects of education and the economy. They strive to create a good future for themselves but recognize that the sociopolitical system does not reward the honest worker. A study conducted by the Economist Intelligence Unit (EIU) ranked the best countries in which to be born in 2013. Of the 80 countries that were evaluated, Ukraine was evaluated as the 78th best place to be born, placed behind countries such as Syria, Pakistan and Bangladesh.[4]

Meaning and Implications

The future is a common theme for teenagers around the world. The unique and valuable insight gained from this study is how the theme of future is connected to disappointment. The future is fragile; young people are placing their hope in social institutions that have been known to fail society.

Ukraine is regularly evaluated to be one of the most corrupt nations in the world.[5] In recent years corruption has gotten worse. A society marked by corruption influences the thinking and behavior of young people. We were surprised to discover from interviewers that campers spoke very little about finding a better life outside of Ukraine.

Going forward, it will be critical for youth workers to help teens manage this obsession about their futures. In addition, it will be critical to equip them with godly ways to manage their frustrations with broken government systems and shattered dreams.

Questions we need to ponder include: What ways can the local churches provide tools to help youth be better students? What valuable skills are necessary to develop in youth for their future? How can God's Word help young people live holy lives in a corrupt system? How can churches be active in giving a larger perspective of what it means to be successful in God's eyes? How can we help youth manage disappointment and gain God's perspective on their situations?

---

[4] "The Lottery of Life". http://www.economist.com/news/21566430-where-be-born-2013-lottery-life (accessed June 22, 2013)

[5] "Corruption Perception Index 2012". http://cpi.transparency.org/cpi2012/results/ (accessed June 22, 2013)

Finding 4
An Underdeveloped Understanding of God

Description

Young people who participated in this research often had an underdeveloped understanding of God. The Ukrainian religious context heavily influences how they understand Christianity. During English camps, young people hear stories from Scripture each night and are taught the good news of Jesus Christ. However, these stories are perceived through the lens of religion in Ukraine, which is characterized by culture and tradition.

Nearly all Ukrainians consider themselves Christians. This stems from an understanding that the label "Christian" implies that a person is neither Muslim nor Jewish, nor practices another world religion. To be Christian is a cultural heritage. Christianity is closely intertwined with Ukrainian national identity. Therefore, the national churches (Greek Catholic, Ukrainian Orthodox) are considered the only "true" Christian church. One student said, "In my circle of friends, no one speaks about God and therefore I don't care at all about a relationship with Him. I see the church as tradition."

Ukrainian young people often agree with the concepts of Christianity presented at camp. Camp spurs students on to attend church more frequently and pray more regularly. Campers "allow" God to indulge in a portion of their lives, but offer him little or no influence in other areas (school, sports, family, and relationships). The Ukrainian students who were interviewed understand the importance of the Bible and believe it is real, yet they have many unresolved spiritual questions. One student said, "I don't want to complicate my life with the church...the relationship I have with God is enough for my life."

DEEP DIVE

Meaning and Implications

This theme is essential to youth ministry's role of guiding young people into a faith-filled relationship with Jesus Christ. As Ukrainian campers hear about life with Christ, they are still equating it with their own experience of traditional Christianity. Ukrainians are receptive to the concept of Jesus as Messiah and many are ready to be redeemed from their sins and go to heaven. But many want this without changing their lives. This challenges our assumption about campers, namely, that students do not understand the gospel when presented to them at camp. The reality is that many youth leave camp understanding the gospel that was presented; however, the gospel presentation has often left out the critical importance of Jesus as Savior and Jesus as Lord in all aspects of life.

Campers need to hear the clear message that God's redeeming work in Christ is meant to infiltrate all areas of their lives. They need to understand the lordship of Jesus and the power of the Holy Spirit to fight temptation. But they need to hear this in a way that is not misinterpreted by their culturally "religious" lenses. Terminology such as prayer, confession, repentance and salvation needs to be clarified in its original, biblical sense. One week at an English Camp does not provide enough time to deconstruct cultural Christianity and fully develop a more biblical Christianity.

The biggest gap in how Ukrainians perceive God is from their lack of understanding that he is Lord over all creation and that he desires our obedience. Churches will need to communicate the purpose and process of sanctification without turning to legalism.

Finding 5
A Different World

Description

Many young people who come to their first English camp expect to practice conversational English and meet Americans. But campers are surprised by something else they experience – it is a different world that they have never felt before. One young person said, "Camp was a great atmosphere, something different than at home." Some of this is due to camp elements such as games, English, and the overall program. In addition, campers explain their surprise when encountering the unique and loving relationships they observed. The Americans and Ukrainians were so friendly that it seemed surreal and artificial. Some attribute this friendliness to the Americans' presence; others attribute it to being at camp. Many of the campers we interviewed were surprised by the Americans' openness and willingness to share their lives. The Americans showed vulnerability and listened to them well. This posture encouraged Ukrainian campers to be more open and vulnerable. Campers enjoyed the experience but felt like they were observing this new world as an outsider.

Many described this community as attractive and appealing but didn't see themselves as part of the fellowship. When they returned home, many kept in contact with camp leaders but didn't engage fully in the church community.

Meaning and Implications

The research revealed that the camp atmosphere is welcoming and loving. In the past youth leaders have believed that having a welcoming and loving environment was enough for campers to feel a part of the community. However, for long-term commitment to belong to a new group, young people must see an ongoing place in the community. When young people did not have a place or a group of friends before camp, they were more likely to join the local church youth group.

In the past, Ukrainian youth leaders ascribed the campers' magnetization to Americans to their use of English or simply to cultural differences. Although this may be partially true, the young people who were surveyed did not mention these characteristics as the reasons why Americans were attractive. They instead mentioned that they were good listeners, open and vulnerable.

Ukrainians must develop more deeply the skills of listening and openness. These qualities are appealing and help build deep and lasting relationships. Americans should be careful not to engage in relationships without intentionally including Ukrainian Christians in order to promote lasting ties to the Ukrainian Christian community after the Americans leave. Relational bonds and loyalty might not otherwise be transferred to the local leaders.

If young people feel like they are observers at camp, they are less likely to become long-term members of the community. Local churches should look for ways to include campers in all aspects of the program. Campers cannot remain casual observers. Leaders should not simply offer camp to campers but rather include them in running camp together. It is important to provide unique "place" and roles for campers and to help them see they are already a part of the community.

Finding 6
No Problems

Description

During the interviews, many young people were quick to say that they did not have any problems. One student stated, "I don't have any problems," but later said he did not have a relationship with his father. Vague and shallow answers were initially given in response to many of the interview questions. They tended to avoid discussing personal issues, particularly about their families. However, as the interviews progressed, many of these young people spoke of issues at school or hinted towards problems with their friends and family. Campers did not view their issues as problems, particularly in comparison with other large-scale problems happening in the country.

Meaning and Implications

Of all of the themes of the research, this theme may be the most surprising and least understood. It is unclear why these Ukrainian young people deny having any problems. Many of the leaders conjectured that they simply did not want to talk about their problems. This initially seemed like a typical pattern for any young person who is asked to open up about life with an older leader. Without developing deep trust, problems are not readily and openly shared. But as the leaders continued to listen, these young people did open up their hearts to a greater extent. It just took time.

This response ("no problems") might point to a cultural tendency to keep problems private. The appearance of having everything put together is important. It is common in Ukraine for serious problems at home or school to never be addressed or discussed. The problems are seen as commonplace. The assumption is that, since everyone has these problems, there is no real need to discuss them. They are not unique. Foreigners have observed this cultural pattern in Ukraine both inside and outside the church. Problems are not discussed and vulnerability is rarely shown. Young people have real problems but do not know how to deal with them. They avoid them and assume that nothing can be done about them.

We need to model healthy relationships and vulnerable openness that leads to spiritual growth and victory over sin. In addition to modeling these qualities, we must create safe places for young people to share their struggles. This includes exhibiting a non-judgmental atmosphere and providing an environment of acceptance. It is critical that leaders ask questions and listen. A camper's first response is not typically the full story. If leaders want to impact the young generation they must listen and not be quick to judge.

Application to Signature Programs

In response to our findings, our English camps will invite parents to camp (if possible or feasible) for an evening program. Or, during camp, church leaders and campers will develop a program to perform for parents and friends in the days following camp. This can take place in the local church in order to create opportunities for the entire church to build relationships with parents and for parents to see the value in these new relationships.

For parents to truly understand the value of the Body of Christ, they must understand the value of a relationship with God. In the past, churches have waited months or years to train youth to share the gospel with family and friends. However, it could be far more impactful to train these youth on how to share their new faith in the days immediately after camp. The Josiah Venture evangelism study "LOOK" is a great tool for new Christians after camp. A mature leader will take the new Christian through "LOOK" after camp to make sure the student fully understands the gospel and also to train them on how to share the gospel with their family and friends.

English Camps will try and reach friends together with the gospel. The gospel message has become too individualistic. The church should make efforts to invite groups of friends to camp together, keep them together at camp, share the gospel with them, and challenge them together to follow Christ.

The gospel presentation has become too narrow and focuses too much on salvation. Salvation is a key part of the gospel, but churches must also teach that Jesus is Lord and King. This emphasis is critical in Ukraine and further develops young people's understanding of God.

Local churches can help parents by helping further their educational goals for their children. The local church can offer tutoring, study groups, skill development, and special training that helps youth become better students and better prepared to enter the work force. When churches focus on development, parents will value the church and want to partner with it. Churches can also teach about Jesus' upside-down kingdom, which places hope in the life that is to come, regardless of the circumstances of life today. When students have a larger worldview and a bigger picture of God's universal plan, it frames an individual's journey for educational goals and career aspirations in an eternal perspective.

Program Experiments

- Parent Day
    Invite parents to camp one night.
    Prepare a special program for parents after camp.
    Try and connect parents to each other and to the church.
- Equipping for sharing the Gospel
    Training all new believers to use "LOOK" to share it with their family and friends
- Building relationships with networks of friends
    Social awareness program in public school
    Develop relationships with friends

> Groups of friends come to English camp
> Challenge groups towards repentance

➢ Develop new English camp talks
> The Josiah Venture Ukraine team will help develop camp themes that are focused on the story of Jesus as Messiah and Jesus as Lord. Ukrainians need to hear the good news that Jesus wants to be Lord of their lives and desires their obedience.

➢ Skill development program
> Photography
> Music
> English
> Football (Soccer)

JV ESTONIA

DEEP DIVE

What makes followers of Christ equippers of youth?

Innar Kruglov, Vahur Kobin, Märt Saar, Kuldar Kaljuste,
Betti Kalamees, Kaspar Nummert, Indrek Tambek

During the past few years in Estonia, we have seen many youth put their faith in to Christ. A lot of them are rooted in Christ and growing as believers. Some of them seem stuck in place, unable to get any further in their walk with God. It almost seems that their view of the Christian life is just to pray the prayer, go to church, listen to Christian music, and await Christ's return.

We believe that this young generation has an enormous potential. It will go to waste if they are not challenged to take more responsibility and ownership of the Great Commission that we received from Jesus. They need to be convicted that this is not something for the "professionals" but for every Christian on a planet. If we could truly capture the essence of the Great Commission, we would see more people trusting Christ every day in our ministries.

To accomplish that we need people who will equip young Christians to fulfill Christ's commission. Right now there is only a limited amount of people who are equipping youth. Part of our challenge is to figure out how to bring more forth and train next generation equippers of youth. This is also the main objective of this our research in Deep Dive. We chose to explore the research question:

What makes followers of Christ equippers of youth?

We interviewed 42 equippers of youth from throughout all of Estonia to discover how they started making disciples, how they were being discipled, and how they are building disciples right now. Among the interviewees were youth leaders, pastors, young leaders in youth group, and small group leaders. All of them were involved in youth ministries. The sample was chosen from our population because they are noted for making great impact in their ministries as leaders, disciple-makers, and equippers. We interviewed them to learn about their characters and experience.

Interviews were convened over the course of two months by our national ministry team including two whom we recruited to help us. We used a common qualitative protocol which was assembled by our national ministry team. The interviews we mostly done face to face, and some of the interviews were done via Skype. Each interview lasted about an hour.

Six key topics surfaced that will help us further in figuring out what makes a follower of Christ an equipper of youth.

Finding 1
Trusting God in Discipleship

Description

In our Deep Dive research in Estonia, a few of the questions were about struggles and failures in ministry. Most (around 75%) of the answers were about issues in disciple-makers or the issues in disciples that made them not want to take next steps in their lives (no further dedication). It often sounded like this: "I'm doing too many things in my life. People are not able to go along with such a pace. I should rather lead them to the world (environment) of Jesus." "He is like a one-day butterfly – this person doesn't have a longer vision and simply lives a careless life. He doesn't want to take responsibility for anything." About 25% of the answers talked about problems in organizing the environments of youth ministry.

When we asked deeper questions about these same struggles, almost all of the interviewees (with one or two exceptions) saw the solution in deepening their own devotion to God or simply trusting God's work over their disciples. "I need to become more like Jesus. I need to do only what I see Father doing". "They belong to God and He is doing the work in them. I need to trust God with them."

Meaning and Implications

When considering this theme alone, no sharp conflicts appear. It's quite healthy that these disciple-makers see most of the solutions to these challenges in their own personal growth or further trust in God. It appears that they need a little more encouragement in order to make sure that the results would come from God. As it became clear in the following theme "How disciple-ships works," some of our response could be informed by a better understanding of how to make disciples.

If we could develop our thinking about goals and measurement of spiritual fruit, it will be easier for the disciple-makers to assess their own hearts and dedication. Clearer ideas about the aims of disciple-making will help them maximize what they are doing and see disciples progressing further while still relying on God's work and not on their own efforts. The question for us is this: How do we teach and prepare disciple-makers so that whenever they experience struggles, they immediately know few steps to take to grow further themselves and effectively lead their struggling disciples?

Finding 2
A disciple-maker must be humble, loving, and obedient

Description

We found that the effective disciple-maker is a people's person. Also disciple maker is forgiving and always looks for the log in his eye before seeking a speck in others. If someone has made a mistake then the disciple maker shows compassionate, as if towards his own brother or sister. He or she will try to describe these situations with compassion. He or she is always speaking of his disciples with a light smile and friendly voice, just as a mother or father would talk of their children.

A disciple-maker is not infallible. Quite often it is a person who has made many mistakes in his life and does not feel ashamed about it, but instead sees his experience as a lesson. When he sees fruit in the disciples he doesn't take it for granted. He knows who the Lord of harvest is. A disciple-maker is like a parent who loves his or her children unconditionally, but at the same time wants them to evolve and strive.

Meaning and Implications

This finding means that a person who loves others is a potential disciple-maker, even if he isn't it at the moment. We should encourage those who are people's people to serve. It appears that they need a lot of affirmation and encouragement. They do not need enormous amounts of extra motivation. It is enough if they are recognized for it and reminded every once in a while why they are doing it. Not much more is needed. It seems also that they do not need new complex tools or ways for doing it, but rather help in making it even simpler and more fruitful.

DEEP DIVE

Perhaps there is a danger in them not being able to discern or apprehend who is ready to be invested in. Their humble and loving hearts are ready to serve sacrificially even when the soil is not really that good. It seems that by fearing to hurt other people and always wanting to be good in the eyes of God, it is difficult for them to say "No" to people, tasks, and situations.

We should set a filter of love-humble-obedient for youth leaders as we ask them to lead. As equippers of youth, we need to be so humble that people notice. We should pay attention to differentiate disciples and disciple-makers more accurately. We should always ask to find out what has causes humbleness and love in people. There should be a platform for disciple-makers to share their "grace stories" to build each other up.

Finding 3
Need for mentoring in churches

Description

The data from our interviews clearly demonstrated that many disciple-makers are not being discipled by anyone themselves. The local church is very important to almost all we interviewed, but there is often no direct mentoring through the local church. Congregations invest a lot into creating environments and platforms and to authorizing the making of disciples, but many are not directly involved. The whole church is not being encouraged to be disciple-makers. Mentoring relationships are not being created.

Many churches are encouraging, talking about it and listening, but their involvement is often limited to just a "pat on the back."

Parallels can also be drawn between the church and family. In Estonian families everyone loves and trusts each other, pats each other on the backs, but rarely does something together. They don't go to cheer the other person on in whatever that person is doing nor do they declare love for each other.

There is caring for what others are doing but the mentality of "I'll be fine on my own" still stands.

The disciple-maker also thinks similar to this. He doesn't feel bitter or disappointed about his home church, but forgives and keeps on loving, quietly wishing the church would change or help more.

It seems that churches are not against discipleship – they are supporting those who do it – but most churches are not disciple-makers themselves.

Meanings and Implications

Based on these interviews we can't assume that churches are on the same page when it comes to discipleship. We should also take care of the disciple-makers, not burden them with discipleship programs and structures in the local church because they might be on their own. We also know that the disciple-maker cares about and loves his church, and that's why he is ready to carry other people's burdens and maintain a good picture of the congregation.

In partnership with churches, we could turn attention to the disciple-makers and ask how the church is prepared to invest in them one-on-one. During interaction with the church, we could bring up ideas about how to encourage more disciple-makers. Definitely we could offer churches our help in raising new disciple-makers.

During partnership meetings with our partner churches, we need to have youth leaders, pastors, and disciple-makers together. We should help pastors raise the right questions which will lead to conversations about disciple-making, knowing that meetings with pastors should be more about discipleship and people, and not as much about other details.

Finding 4
Lack of strategic trajectory

Description

This theme was chosen due to a recurring pattern throughout our interviews. The main problem that came out in many different ways was a "lack of trajectory." There was considerable talk about many aspects of "lack of trajectory." Firstly, we ran into the "dreams are big" factor, which we recognize is a big problem in Estonia. We often dream of ideas and projects and don't think of the actual situation itself and the resources that are at hand. This leads to the problem of using all our energy on planning and visioning, but failing to see any progress, or seeing very little progress. Therefore, we as disciple-makers have to make more of an effort to make change happen, so we could have noticeable progress in disciple making. Secondly, a common problem we recognize is that we try to see change in the church but do not actually concentrate on the disciples and the progress they are making.

Meanings and Implications

There were two topics that surfaced through this finding. The first is our emphasis on being event-focused. By this we meant that we concentrate on putting together youth events, youth nights, and other activities. This usually brings quantity, but not quality. Quality comes more from intimate conversations and time that is spent with disciples. We should aim for this instead of trying to see progress through an endless line of events.

Another problem with events we heard is that people are often very skilled at being critical of others. When our focus is putting together events, it leads to arguments and negative experiences, which also have a negative impact on disciples. We should not see this kind of interaction, but rather the love and grace of God.

The second topic that emerged from this finding was the lack of "deep reflection." We saw that we often duplicate events, and do not always deeply discuss the importance and relevance of the event when looking at the context of the subject in the Bible. This illuminated the problem of people lacking knowledge, misunderstanding the Bible and its content. This often leads to misunderstandings and false teachings.

This theme is really important to our ministry, because we frequently do not challenge ourselves to look deeply into the reasons why our progress is not as fast as it actually could and should be. Deep Dive, as a concept, is a totally new approaching to dealing with the problems Estonian ministries might have and do have. So this way of interviewing definitely brought out the standard faults when it comes to Estonian ministries.

What should we from now on and pay attention to in response to what we learned from this theme? The main thing to take from this is to think deeply about our actions and activities and really concentrate on doing what we have to do, rather than just visioning better and better plans in order to do something. Process and deep reflection together are the key factors to take from this.

Also we need to be more critical about the decisions we make and about the things we think are right, because we often fool ourselves into thinking something is good, when actually it may be the anchor pulling us down.

Finding 5
Replicate your experience

Description

This theme came through the interviews clearly. Almost everybody thought of discipleship as replicating your own way of living. Yet making the disciple requires reliance on God instead of the disciple-maker. This idea means that there are themes from a disciple-maker's life which are important to emulate or avoid. This theme has 4 sub-themes:

a. Constant change
b. Upgrade yourself
c. Tolerance
d. Don't let emotions get in the way

Constant change evolved into a sub-theme, because we heard the same point in many interviews. This point was brought out especially well by one of the youth leaders: "The moment, when I don't change anymore, is the moment I'm not relevant anymore. For youth, a leader is only attractive when the leader is constantly changing. That inspires the youth to change."

Also under this sub-theme, we heard that constant change is important for being able to identify with youth. Some have seen the effectiveness of responsiveness in their disciple-making. Identifying with youth is important because a lot of the new generation of youth have a very different way of thinking. It's hard to connect with that without being very conscious. The greater your difference in age, the more you have to acknowledge this point in making a disciple of that person.

Upgrading yourself was categorized as a sub-theme because 99% of the interviewees said something about upgrading yourself through schooling or ongoing training. The interviewees pointed out that it is very important to be a fresh and constantly learning in order to stay relevant for youth. Also, we heard that it is so important to spend more time with God because this gives you the most intimate experiences. Those are essential for getting the most out of one-on-one time with the disciple.

Tolerance was also an important point for many interviewees. This was talked about because many times there will be situations where you will be disappointed or hurt because the disciple will make mistakes. When we let their mistakes get to us, the strength of relationship may suffer.

Our conclusion is that disciple-makers have to be ready for everything and should not presume that only may you hurt the disciple, but the disciple might hurt you as well. It was mentioned that when you don't expect anything for yourself, then you love the disciple-making relationship the most. This is not from everyone, but a few felt that way.

Also, not letting emotions get in the way appeared to be a key element in the whole disciple-making process. We find ourselves in situations where the worst can be brought out of us. In situations like this it is important to remind yourself of the role you have in the relationship. We need to show the love of Christ, not show the love the world has. This can be brought out of people in situations that are most difficult for them—for example, in sports when people are competitive or in detailed work when people get cranky when they are interrupted. Keep in mind that we are changed by God. Let that be seen by your disciple!

Finding 6
How discipleship works

Description

We discovered that we can't assume that every Christian servant in Estonia will have clear understanding of what discipleship exactly is or how it works. However, most of the respondents actually talked about similar elements and qualities when asked about the deeper beliefs, character, and love behind any work with other people. In one way or another, they hinted at the great mission command (Matthew 28) and the importance of spiritual one-on-one work. Some of the disciple-makers do it intentionally, other's do not.

> You can't just take the decision that now you're going make him or her a disciple, there's has to be love and friendship.
>
> Discipling has to be a calling.
>
> The discipling term is rather an American thing. Terminology changes, but the content is the same.
>
> I don't like the word discipling at all, I think it's rather soul-care we're talking about.

Meaning and Implications

The difference in statements shows quite clearly that the interviewees have very different ideas about what discipleships really means and what should be its main applications. At the same time, interviewees expressed quite similar values. Ministers in Estonia are often afraid to adopt

"American" projects for fear of losing a clear and right motivation. They want stay natural in their ministry, but they also want to see results and encourage next steps for the people God has placed in their lives and ministries.

We were surprised to hear most interviewees say that you can't take your disciple further than you have gone yourself, and that you can't teach what you don't live out yourself. Some thought about the people in their ministries as disciples, but for others discipleship was quite separate area altogether.

There are many servant-hearted people in Estonia who have a deep commitment level to their calling but who don't see discipleship itself as a very important part of what they do. Or, they have vague and general ideas about it. Of course, some of them just do it under a different name (e.g., soul-care). Therefore, the people who are struggling to discover their calling might fail to become disciple-makers at all because they don't see it as something natural that they can submit to in their everyday lives.

In the future we should really value discipleship a lot more in Estonia. The question is, how? What would the ministries do and teach differently? How can we get rid of any doubt that disciple-making should be something every single believer should do?

We should give people the right look at discipleship – that on one hand it has to be quite intentional and that it is vital to measure some steps in the followers lives, but on the other hand it will have to have very personal and natural features like calling, love, friendship, and an invitation to visit in homes.

Application to Signature Programs

In the light of the findings we can definitely learn something and apply the knowledge to real-life ministry here in Estonia. Here are some of the things that we could apply:

It is very important to examine youth leaders as you ask them to lead because you cannot assume that the youth leader has the qualities in him or her that you are looking for. Leading by example is one of the things that cannot fall into the category of clichés. Every good disciple-maker needs to be humble. We should pay more attention to how lead because people will follow our example. If we don't make disciples then the youth who we work with won't do it either. In a way, wimpy Christians produce wimpy Christians.

The word "discipleship" has been carelessly thrown around in Christian circles for the past five years or so. This is why the term has lost some of the original meaning. We hear Christians say that all Christians should make disciples, and somehow they assume that all Christians are already making disciples. But this is just not the truth. To avoid this dangerous pitfall we need to make this process more intentional and strategic.

Our findings show that Christians who are really making

disciples are very humble and loving in character. This research has set us on a new journey to find out what has caused this kind of humility and love to be grown in them.

The basis of our ministry has been partnerships with local churches. And that has been mostly through the youth leader. We've seen that this can be shallow because often the pastor and the youth leader might not be on the same page when it comes to youth ministry or discipleship. This is why all the partnership meetings should involve also the pastor or the elders from the church. And during the meetings we want to help the pastors to raise the right first questions. For example we don't want to talk with them about camp details before we talk about discipleship and the heart of their church.

We need to make sure that the people we lead through different materials are having a great relationship with God. And in the light of that, trust that God is bringing forth the growth and fruit in them. This is how we can make sure that they are hearing what God is telling them. One of the things we need to do is revisit material Shift 1|9 to see from where the fruit actually comes from.

We often like to share success stories. We expect that we can best learn from successes and somehow replicate them. It is good to realize that there are many failure stories as well. What we learn from these failures are often even more valuable sources of wisdom. We also need to use these stories to teach, guide, and motivate different youth leaders.

During the past five years we have had a lot of interns coming to serve us and mostly we have seen them as servants. It would be much more helpful to see them as disciple-makers and expect them to make disciples. Interns are very valuable workers. They have all the time in the world to focus on discipleship and we should more put it to use.

We also need to be thinking of the disciple-makers that we

interviewed and how can we mobilize them, how can we help them to equip others better, and how to keep them motivated. Disciple-makers need to have a strategy or a plan for discipleship. Discipleship could be more fruitful many times over if disciple-makers had a specific direction, plan, and strategy in mind. This is something we need to bring to disciple-makers. A very good and helpful tool would be the SonLife strategy which helps disciple-makers plan ahead and recognize where people are in their walk with God and how to challenge them further.

Program Experiments

For further findings and to text our present findings, we can try the following experiments.

- ➢ We would like to have two teams working together on something. One has no time to plan and strategize, the other has one hour time to plan and strategize. We'd like to see which team performs better. Maybe it comes out that free style works just fine; we'd like to see how that would work.

- ➢ One of the experiments we'd like to try is a worship night with failure stories as testimonies and see how God's grace and wisdom would come out of that. It would be interesting to see if the failure stories build people up as much a success stories.

- ➢ We'd like to try micro seminars. We don't have to create a big event to get the people together. There are big events happening already anyways. But what if we could be there and use that time and space as a platform for equipping other Christians? We don't need to spend all that time and energy to get people together when they are already gathering.

- To see how natural discipleship is to disciple-makers, we'd like to take them out on a picnic with some of the youth. We won't plan any teaching program, just a very relaxing environment. And there we will observe who is actually making disciples and who is not, who has it as a life style, and who has it as a program in their lives.

- The last experiment we'd like to try is the "shadow day". We want young Christians to follow strong disciple-makers throughout the whole day and just observe how they live their life, how they are at work, and how they interact with their family and friends. Hopefully the young Christians will learn that discipleship is very natural and it's not a program. Later they can evaluate and talk about the things the young Christian observed.

JV CZECH REPUBLIC

How are young leaders grown and developed in the local church? How are they growing and developing new leaders?

Bogdan Lach, Martina Pixová, Tomáš Samiec, David Rajca, Jonathan Rosen, Josh Nelson, Daniel Johnson, Rob Chestnut, Dušan Drabina, Milan Michalko, Marek Slansky

Křesťanská akademie mladých (KAM) is a nonprofit organization in the Czech Republic, serving under the umbrella of Josiah Venture whose mission is "to equip young Christian leaders to fulfill Christ´s commission."

Dave Patty, the founder of Josiah Venture, was called to serve in the Czech Republic in 1993, only a couple of years after the fall of Communism. The churches were oppressed, operating underground, and in survival mode at the time. Youth programs remained undeveloped, and outreach to youth was virtually unheard of.

Because this Communist regime was one of the toughest in Europe, the nation went through two decades of "normalization," when everybody who stood out from the crowd was looked down upon and was subject to persecution by the police. As one can imagine, this kind of environment did not foster a healthy view of and commitment to leadership. Unfortunately, many of these patterns of behavior and perceptions of leadership have remained with us even after many years of freedom.

Now, 23 years after the fall of Communism and despite the fact that a whole new generation of young people has grown up free from Communism, the Czech Republic is still considered one of the most atheistic nations in the world. However, a recent survey about faith and beliefs among high school students revealed that young people are more open today to religion and belief in the supernatural than in the past. Despite this new openness, the church is challenged to reach young people with the message of the gospel and develop them into mature followers of Christ. Due to this reality, churches and Christian organizations are plagued by a lack of young leaders. Even though we have seen thousands of professions of faith over the last 20 years, we struggle to find young people willing to step into leadership.

After observing this trend for some time, we decided that the Deep Dive project could help us understand what we are experiencing and what changes we need to make. Therefore, the focus of this project was to determine how best to see a new generation of young leaders built up in the church.

We selected the following two research questions:

How are young leaders grown and developed in the local church?
How are they growing and developing new leaders?

We identified 123 young leaders from 47 cities across the country and from 13 different denominations. This group consisted of either formal leaders of youth groups or those with potential to become leaders in the future.

The KAM leadership team appointed and trained 11 interviewers from our staff to be able to lead conversations according to the protocol, which consists of 13 sets of questions. Between December 2012 and May 2013 our team interviewed 45 young leaders in person or through a Skype call. Each interview took 45-75 minutes.

As we conducted interviews and analyzed the data from our interviews, two large themes stood out to us. Each of these larger themes contained sub-themes. By far the largest theme emerging from this study was the importance of leadership development taking place within the context of relationship. The second larger theme was the difference between what we assumed the local church was doing and what they actually were doing on behalf of the development of young leaders. We also discovered a few other factors affecting the leadership effectiveness of young leaders. But the above two themes and the way they are inter-related forms the backbone of this study.

Theme A
Leadership Development Takes Place within the Context of Relationship

Without question, one of the overarching themes that surfaced repeatedly and in various forms throughout our study was how important relationships are to leadership development. When young leaders discussed what they felt they needed or what had been most beneficial in their development as leaders, they almost always mentioned personal attention and direction from others. This forces us to take a closer look at the ways relational leadership contributes to the development of young leaders.

Finding 1
Personal Attention

Description

When we asked respondents about their path to leadership, "What helped you the most on your path to becoming a good leader?" the response of one of those interviewed, "Having someone to learn from," was typical of a large portion of those interviewed. Many claimed that personal care, leadership, and feedback were significant to their development as leaders. Most of them also noted that they first became involved in ministry because of a personal invitation from another leader.

Yet then when we asked the question: "If your church or denomination focused on leadership development for the next five years what would you dream about in this area of ministry? What would be ideal in your opinion?" Often the answers included recommendations such as organizing seminars, putting on conferences, or preparing some kind of program. This was a striking disconnect from their personal experience.

We also discovered that many young leaders were not actually currently experiencing personal care or leadership. They were invited into ministry, perhaps even mentored for a time, but once they held a formal position of leadership they often no longer received personal care and direction. Churches sometimes were willing to pay for them to attend events or seminars, but did not take an active role in their development.

Meaning and Implications

We should admit that as we conducted this study we felt the Spirit of God actually convicting us as a team. We recognized that personal attention and discipleship played a key role in all of our lives. But when we think about developing the next generation, we often subconsciously tend towards ministry and leadership development through programs or events. We began to recognize in ourselves a collective and subconscious doubt about the efficacy of discipleship and the principles of multiplication. It also seems that churches doubt their own ability to develop leaders. They do not appear to prioritize it. There are many options for sending young leaders through leadership training, but it seems that they rarely experience personal care and development within the church itself.

We can already see the consequences of these "one off" forms of education. Most Bible schools and seminaries founded on an intellectual and impersonal foundation are running into a lack of interested students. Our research shows that in the lives of young leaders, personal interest and personal leadership play a key role. They are both attractive and important for the personal growth of the leader.

Therefore, on the basis of this study, we then make the following recommendation: As leaders, let's look for other potential leaders (disciples) in our various spheres of influence and give them personal attention. This may come through giving them specific challenges, encouragement, help, and direction. This style of ministry will be effective for developing future generations of leaders.

We are also challenged to ask the question about how we can make leadership training within KAM fit young leaders' needs for personal attention and direction. We are providing much in the way of leadership training, but in doing so are we actually keeping churches from getting personally involved? How can we better partner with churches to make sure young leaders are receiving consistent and personal leadership training in and through the church?

DEEP DIVE

Finding 2
Examples

Description

We found that another main influence on the development of young leaders is by watching others who are further ahead and learning from them. Those interviewed noted that seeing real people "live out" leadership principles in front of them helped them to understand how to "live out" these principles of leadership in their own context. Models take abstract ideas and bring them to life for these young leaders.

Respondents also mentioned that it was important to have models that were relationally close. When speaking about models, most young leaders could think of specific people who influenced their life by giving them opportunities to serve and by being willing to spend time with them and care for them personally.

Meaning and Implications

This finding confirms our conviction that how we lead is just as important for those following as the decisions we make. In fact, these findings should encourage us to remember that sometimes we need to make decisions simply because of the example we set for others. Also, it reminds us that we need to be looking for potential future leaders and bringing them along with us as we lead. They need to see how their leader is living as much, if not more, than acquiring the specific skills to run the ministry.

These data also seem to reveal that a variety of models are needed. Some leaders mentioned models which had no formal leadership role but who were worth emulating in some aspect of their lives. Respondents also look up to those who have ministry capabilities and learn from them. This presents a challenge to us as leaders to recognize that we cannot be an example for everyone in everything. We should be aware of our limitations and perhaps invite others who are models in other areas to work with us.

The findings also reveal that young leaders are attentive to the entire lives of those who are leading. We need to keep in mind that the example we set by our lifestyle is being followed just as much as what we accomplish in ministry.

Realizing the importance that young leaders place on having models in their lives should cause us as KAM to think through how to become models for the youth leaders that we are working with. We should ask ourselves the question, "Are we preparing them for the ministry they need to do or are we doing it for them?"

Another one of our questions relates to the role of formal Christian education and training. Bible schools, seminaries and internship programs are all struggling to recruit new students. Even programs that focus on providing models for these young leaders are still struggling to keep up their enrollment. This makes us ask what we need to change to meet the needs of more young leaders. How can we make models available to them in their current situations without asking them to leave their current context?

Another area that we could potentially work on as KAM is setting an example for people by caring about them personally. What would it communicate to churches and leaders if we connected with them regularly just to encourage them and find out how they are doing?

Finding 3
Sharing Life

Description

Experiencing and sharing life together is also one of the keys to leadership development. This is "on the go" discipleship, where leaders and disciples do not just meet to discuss something and learn, but learn together in the real world. "You can't just teach through a series on leadership, you have to live it together with them," one respondent said. "All the guys in my small group will be leaders in some way." Those surveyed mentioned how they were most impacted by personal time with the leader far more than meetings about strategy or vision. This requires the leader to be a living example, build a relationship with them, and spend time together.

Having an open house is one way to share life together. One leader shared, "I saw [the leader] open his home to me and share his life, and that's impacted how we do our ministry here." A lot is learned without being specifically taught. Some also expressed this influence as starting from before belief and progressing through to mature faith. Therefore, we were able to see that young leaders are impacted and developed as they work, rest, serve, and in general experience life alongside older more mature brothers and sisters.

Meaning and Implications

These data suggest that we cannot just create more programs for churches or young leaders to follow in order to consider them discipled and developed as leaders. We will have to walk through ministry development with them. It means that although programs can have some effect, the true key to leadership development is much more personal. We need to help the church see that the older members need to be involved with the younger members' lives and not just meet with them once in a while to talk about life.

One of the ways we may be able to specifically help churches in this area is by encouraging the more mature members of the church to build relationships with specific students in the youth group or church. This may also mean that college students are not the most effective youth group leaders because they are away five days a week. It may mean that they need to develop as leaders in their university town. Life-on-life discipleship requires more than just the weekend of ministry.

One of the unique challenges these findings provide for us as KAM is to find ways to model life-on-life discipleship and encourage churches to do the same. As we put together trainings and conferences, one of the questions we will have to ask ourselves is how will this promote discipleship in the context of real life? How can we design trainings and teaching to be compatible with this idea of sharing life together? In what ways could we as KAM exemplify this as we build relationships with local churches and leaders?

Finding 4
Encouraging Relationships

Description

We set out to understand how young leaders are growing in the local church, and discovered that having encouraging relationships did not directly develop young leaders but played a significant role in the leader's continued willingness to lead and his or her desire to grow. "I want someone else to be accountable to—to ask how I'm doing, to encourage me, to pray with me and for me." To the question, What have you valued the most in your own development as a leader? we heard, "I knew someone was with me, someone behind my back [had my back]." "I love to go through the process [getting trained] together with other people."

To the question, What have you valued the most in your own development as a leader? we heard answers like, "People challenging me to do things outside my comfort zone." To the question, What has kept you engaged in your leadership through the difficult or challenging times? we commonly heard, "I'd say it's encouragement from other people," "the support of people I'm leading and their gratitude kept me engaged...good friendships, sharing lives refuels me." In these relationships the love of Christ is manifested.

Meaning and Implications

This study challenges the concept many of us have had, that a leader is a lone ranger who can get it done all on his own. Instead, we see that he actually needs a web of relationships around him to persevere in leadership. Clearly it is not enough for a church or group to receive leadership, allow someone to lead, or invite someone to lead. There must be feedback and encouragement. Silence communicates, "We do not care, and we are not grateful," whether or not it is true. To assume young leaders have encouraging relationships is foolish, naive, and dangerous. The Bible speaks to this when it says that if we are to "love one another earnestly from a pure heart," then we must "spur each other on to love and good deeds."

This information also reveals that leadership training is about more than developing someone's skills. They may have all the right skills or training, but if they don't feel support from friends or superiors they probably will not continue to serve. The research also indicates that the isolation of leadership actually discourages some from being willing to take on roles of leadership.

Older leaders need to be trained. Cultures of encouragement need to be developed in the local church. Young leaders need to be connected to fellow leaders, young and old. If the goal is to develop young leaders, then we need also to develop their communities (those they are leading, peers, and other leaders) in their regions or fields). There must also be development for leaders of leaders in the area of top-down encouragement (from superiors). Developing a young leader focuses on the specific individual in part, but focusing on developing the young leader's community of encouraging relationships can cause him or her to not merely develop but thrive.

These findings also raise some strategic questions. Is it better to invite a team of people into pioneering work or a gifted leader? How can we help young leaders be encouraged by the approval of others and yet not be dependent on it in order to lead?

Conclusion

Despite some of our pictures of the ideal leader who becomes great against all odds, our research indicates that leadership development takes place within the context of relationship. Young leaders need personal attention, examples to follow, the chance to share life with others, and encouraging relationships to grow and persevere as leaders.

These findings actually challenge where we tend to put a great deal of our efforts. We tend to provide a great deal of training, seminars, and skill development. But young leaders in Czech need relationships. Young leaders feel somewhat alone. They want someone to care about them and take the time to listen and encourage them.

Based on the results of this study, it seems that churches and Christian leaders need to address a few different issues that may be slowing down personal leadership development. First, our interviews show that leadership development is as much about care and interest as it is about acquiring great skills or knowledge. Thus, just about anyone can contribute to leadership development if they will take time and show interest in the potential of young leaders. Also, these findings seem to indicate that we often lack the conviction and vision for personal leadership development. This leads us to ask these questions: How do we help people move from development of programs to development of leaders? How do the sins of fear and control contribute to a lack of willingness to develop new leaders and release them into ministry?

Theme B
Church Expectations vs. Church Investment

Because we were trying to determine how leaders are developed within the context of the local church, we were curious about the average young leaders' experience with the church. In general, our data suggest that churches tend to have a narrow understanding of leadership (what is required, what young leaders are trying to accomplish, what they are allowed to influence, etc.). We also saw that church leaders rarely personally invest in the personal development of young leaders. This led us to see a tension between what is expected of young leaders and the resources or support that they are given to fulfill those expectations.

Finding 5
The Church Community Shapes Definitions of Leadership

Description

The interviews showed that when young leaders step into leadership, they often step into roles that are already clearly defined by the church. We found that churches tend to view leadership in terms of a role or position as opposed to influence or development of others. In general, leaders are expected to organize programs and make sure the ministry is taking place instead of developing students or young leaders personally. The expectation of churches is that the programs organized by the leaders will do the work of discipleship.

We also discovered that young leaders tend to wait on the invitation of others, specifically church leadership, before they step into roles of greater responsibility. A common response to the question how this person became a leader sounded like, "I was invited by the pastor or elder board to lead." We saw that their willingness to step into leadership is largely influenced by the affirmation and approval of others.

Meaning and Implications

These findings lead us to conclude that few leaders get into ministry unless invited by those they perceive to be ahead of them. Young people may believe that the church determines who is fit for leadership and who is not. Since the church ties leadership to a specific role, it also limits the amount of leadership roles the church sees as necessary. These findings also remind us that few people decide to become leaders on their own. We should affirm the potential we see in them and invite them forward.

For KAM, this could mean that unless church leadership is in agreement with the roles we invite young leaders to occupy, these roles may be seen as invalid. We may also find that our definition of a fruitful leader through KAM might be in opposition to the local church if the church primarily views youth leaders as organizers of youth programs.

One of the areas where our assumptions should be challenged based on these results is that telling someone how to be a good leader (through book, seminar, etc.) does not often help the person get started on the path toward leadership. It seems that there needs to be closer personal interaction and connection on a local level.

A significant challenge presented by these findings is to help churches expand their vision for informal leadership. We should also ask how we could cast a greater vision for informal leadership and expand the opportunities for young people to be given leadership challenges? How could we as KAM to help local churches support and validate the leadership roles we are offering to young leaders?

DEEP DIVE

Another way to potentially help churches could be by helping them identify potential in young leaders and craft informal roles of leadership for them. In partnership with churches, we should also think through how we define what it means to be a leader.

Finding 6
Voids of Leadership Development within the Local Church

Description

The youth we interviewed mentioned that they are given the responsibility of leading youth groups, small groups, clubs, and such. But many of them noted that they are not receiving any personal direction, leadership, or care themselves. They feel that at times the most interaction they receive with church leadership is when they are reprimanded for mistakes.

Many youth leaders admit that they search for leadership resources outside their church. They look to YouTube, books, online readings, "outsourced personal leadership" from other churches, and attendance of leadership seminars or conferences to receive mentoring and guidance.

In general, we discovered that from the perspective of young leaders most churches lack a clear understanding of or strategy for leadership development.

Meaning and Implications

One of the dangers that we face as a result of this lack of understanding of leadership development is that young people are often not led to seek God's leading in their life. They are simply told to try out ministry without much in the way of guidance or direction. This can lead to leadership that is primarily utilitarian in nature. Young leaders simply try to do their best, not always understanding how they should do what they are doing or why.

This also leads us to the conclusion that many youth leaders feel alone in what they are trying to accomplish. This may give us some insight into the trend we see for youth leaders leaving youth ministry at such young ages. If they have not felt led into the position by God and do not feel church support for their work, it is difficult to persevere in leadership. Also, because church leadership is often not connected very well to these young leaders and their ministries, new leaders step into leadership positions and are forced to forge their own path all over again.

Perhaps one of the most frightening implications of this trend is that despite all of the work that has gone into teaching about leadership development, it is still not happening. As a parachurch organization, we have to ask ourselves how we can promote development of leaders within the church itself. It may be possible that we are contributing to the problem by providing so much leadership training outside the context of the local church.

The warning is here for us and all leaders. Effective leadership development is about more than giving someone responsibility. It involves investment, relationship, and perhaps most importantly our willingness to help potential leaders learn to sense God's leading for themselves.

One of our challenges is in understanding why this is happening. In theory, many have been taught that leadership development is best done in the context of relationship and real life, but very few are actually living this out. So these findings raise other questions: Are older leaders too busy to invest in this way? Are they not interested in leadership development? Are they worried that they don't have anything to offer younger leaders? Perhaps in discovering the answers to some of these questions we will know better how and where to apply our energy in leadership development as an organization.

DEEP DIVE

Conclusion

These findings challenge us as both leaders within the local church and as leaders of a Para-church organization to face a difficult reality that young leaders are often discouraged and feel alone in the various ministry tasks they have been assigned. Despite many of our sincere efforts, young leaders don't appear to feel supported. Perhaps one element of this reality is that young leaders have not been pointed in the right direction to the care they need. People will ultimately never meet all of our needs. So, to some degree we probably need to do a better job of receiving what we need from God and encouraging young leaders to do the same. Yet, we need to also see an increase in our commitment to care for and develop young leaders as well as expand our definition of leadership beyond that of simply a formal role. These two steps may be risky and scary, but Jesus shows us that this type of vulnerability is how leaders are developed. He shows us that opening ourselves up to disappointment and hurt not only expresses that our ultimate trust is in God, but it gives others space to learn and grow.

Additional Themes

We also discovered a few other factors that contribute to leadership development within the local church that are not as clearly connected to the two larger topics.

CZECH REPUBLIC

Finding 7
Leadership Development in a Real Life Ministry Context

Description

One type of question that we posed during our Deep Dive Research Project was this: What in your opinion is the best way to help develop a young person into a leader? What personally helped you the most in your own journey to becoming a good leader? One of the strong undertones that came out in the answers was that an important element in their journey towards becoming a leader was the opportunity to grow within the context of real ministry or work. It seems that good leaders experience something that we could call "an opportunity to get their feet wet." This was especially effective when the opportunity to try out ministry was combined with personal leadership and care.

Interestingly, there was no mention of seminars, conferences, or books on leadership in these responses when they spoke of what was crucial to their development as leaders. This absence was surprising to us because we know that many of these young leaders have used these resources.

Meaning and Implications

Our research again confirms the strategy of leadership and discipleship that Jesus lived. Yet this strategy continues to be one that we forget to apply. Jesus gave his disciples the chance to get their feet wet when he sent them out and commanded them, "Do not go among the Gentiles or enter any town of the Samaritans," (Matthew 10:5). We can also clearly see how Jesus gave his followers space to fail as well, which also contributed to the process of growth. "Whenever it seizes him, it throws him to the ground. He foams at the mouth, gnashes his teeth and becomes rigid. I asked your disciples to drive out the Spirit, but they could not," (Mark 9:18).

It also means that true leadership development may be more difficult to measure than we would like. Someone doesn't become a leader simply by reading a book or attending a class. There is an element of experience that simply can't be taught in a classroom. If the ministry of a leader is not bearing fruit in practical ministry, then he or she doesn't have anywhere else to invite another potential young leader. For that reason, we surmise that development is relegated to a ministry "school."

If we are going to develop future leaders, we need to invite them to get involved in practical ministry. As leaders we have to come to terms with the fact that new young leaders will not be interested in getting involved in exactly the same ministry as we are already doing. In that case, the challenge then is for us, in the interest of developing future leaders, to change our ministry and come alongside the younger generation as they serve. The research indicates that if new leaders go through this kind of process, they will become stronger leaders.

There is also a deeper spiritual question that is raised by these discoveries. Why are we so inclined, at least in Czech, to teach and lead seminars on leadership? Do we lack opportunities to give to young leaders to get their feet wet? What would need to change in order to see lots of new practical opportunities for young leaders?

Finding 8
The Role of Calling in Leadership Development

Description

We found that a sense of calling or lack thereof also has a profound impact on how young leaders view and approach their ministry, especially over a long period of time. Yet, the challenge that we discovered for most young leaders is that many churches don't tend to lead young people to think in terms of their calling. Instead, they focus on tasks and responsibilities.

We also discovered that those who felt some sense of calling upon their lives experienced that call in their personal relationship with God. Yet, the call did not take place in a vacuum. It came through opportunities to serve and feeling a sense of God's leading and direction as they served.

We also noticed that those who spoke about having received a calling viewed their ministry differently. One respondent explained, "I read 2 Corinthians 4:1 (Therefore, since through God's mercy we have this ministry, we do not lose heart) coming back to Czech and I knew this was from God." Those experiencing a sense of call generally had more hope and took more steps to pursue that calling (training, school, and ministry opportunities).

Meaning and Implications

These findings confirmed the importance of designing guided ministry opportunities for young people. They don't necessarily need to lead a big program, but they need opportunities to serve and be encouraged to process this experience with others and personally seek out what God might have for them. It is fairly intuitive that young people need to try out ministry before they can decide whether or not they will continue in service, but we need to remember that God's leading needs to be an integral piece of the process as well.

It surprised us how many young leaders are actually serving without a deeper sense of calling. They often stepped into leadership because no one else was willing or the church asked them to do it. This brings further understanding to the trend that we see of youth leaders leaving youth ministry when they get married. They tend to serve more out of a sense of duty than out of sensing God's leading or call. Some may equate the invitation of church leadership to serve to be the same as God's call, but this still lacks a sense of personal conviction.

A significant challenge presented by these findings is to seek out a better understanding of this whole topic of calling and how to lead young people to seek out God's call upon their lives. Questions that we will have to wrestle with are whether or not this process is best fostered and led by the church and what role a Para-church organization can play in this process.

These findings also challenge us to view the process of leadership development as more than simply training young leaders to develop ministry skills. We actually need to ask the question, how can we lead young leaders to actually seek out God's call on their lives? In what ways can we foster this by giving them opportunities to serve? How do we best guide those experiences so that it is not just about filling a hole or learning a skill, but actually becomes an environment in which they learn about their gifts and can seek God's leading for their lives?

Finding 9
Spiritual Habits

Description

Another one of the key themes, which appeared during the Deep Dive interviews, was a need for developing the spiritual habits of new believers who come to faith through Josiah Venture programs. Some of the respondents stressed the importance of in-depth studies of the Bible.

We also saw that young leaders learn spiritual habits and disciplines while being with others who practice them. Young leaders often learn skills for leading others or programs, but their spiritual habits might be neglected. Despite the fact that both churches and organizations are aware of the importance of developing people's spiritual lives, respondents often did not mention this as an aspect of spiritual leadership.

Meaning and Implications

This study could perhaps reveal a view of leadership that does not involve a person's entire life. When compared with Jesus' life it seems that Jesus didn't draw a distinction between the importance of spiritual habits and leadership skills when leading others. This may reveal that traditional views of leadership have more to do with certain skills than a certain way of living.

The best example of care for new believers can be found in the ministry of Jesus Christ. We need to have the mentality of Jesus. Discipleship is about sharing life with those whom we are discipling. There are two important aspects to this process; there is a need for a deep biblical study and there is also a need for reflection upon spiritual progress.

Our programs are focused on evangelism and reaching out to unchurched kids. The assumption of our team is that the spiritual growth and development of healthy spiritual habits is the role of the local church. The Deep Dive research helped us understand that this can become a bottleneck. We will try to follow up with the partnering local churches and keep asking them about the care of new believers who came to Christ through JV programs.

In terms of leadership development, this means that we will have to learn to model not just how to lead programs effectively, but also how to develop spiritual habits. Also, it forces us to ask the question, what about our spiritual habits? If this is something that is not being caught, how much do we need to evaluate our own lives in this area?

We will also need to help prepare churches for the fact that developing spiritual habits in young believers takes time. It is something young leaders need to see modeled, not just hear about.

Finding 10
Managing the Tension between Ministry and Life

Description

As we interviewed young leaders and asked them about some of the challenges they face, a consistent response was that they are not sure how to best manage their time. Many explained how they faced the challenge of only leading as volunteers while trying to balance the demands of school and/or work as well. Despite their desire to invest more time in their ministry, they don't know how. Those we interviewed relayed how much internal stress this caused for them, especially the college students who spend on average 2-3 months per year just on their finals. They want to make sure they do well in school, but they feel that the time they are investing in school takes away from their ability to invest into their ministry.

One young leader interviewed gave a response characteristic of many saying, "I need to learn time management skills. I can't seem to get it all done." It seems that leaders feel that they consistently have to make choices between their ministry and the other requirements of life.

Meaning and Implications

The reality of this tension helps us better to understand the trend we see for many leaders to serve for a certain period of time before the pressures of work and family take them away from service. At the same time though, we find that there are some young leaders who can persevere through these challenges. These develop great character and leadership qualities that they take with them to overall leadership within the church.

Due to the reality that these young leaders are serving as volunteers alongside school and work and are often receiving very little personal benefit, we should think through how we can help these young leaders. (Many, in fact, invest not only their time but their finances.) They feel as if they aren't doing enough for their ministries. But they are doing their best. As a result, we should exercise sensitivity in the challenges and advice we give to young leaders. This might also lead us to challenge more adults with a little more stable routine to get involved and help these young leaders out in small ways. Particularly, it would seem to make sense to recruit more adults to personally disciple students.

Sadly, these findings may be more indicative of more widespread cultural factors. Young leaders are struggling with having time to give to ministry, studies, and personal relationships in the way that they envision and desire. We have to ask if leaders ahead of them are doing any better. In general, it seems that we are missing a healthy view of and framework for lay ministry. Many leaders feel that ministry is incompatible with their family or work life.

Therefore, they have to add ministry on the side. We need to ask, how can we build a healthier picture of the integration between ministry and life? If we are to model this, to what extent have we dealt with this issue in our own lives?

Also, these findings present unique findings for us as people in full time ministry. We need to ask ourselves hard questions. Are we asking young leaders to make sacrifices we are unwilling to make? Are our expectations for what the ministries of young leaders should look like realistic?

Conclusions

This project presented a significant challenge for our team, in conducting interviews, analyzing data, and describing our findings. Despite these challenges, this project was significant not only for what we discovered, but for how it challenged and shaped us as a team. One leader noted how the interview process actually caused him to recognize how he often thinks of leadership development in terms of programs as opposed to personal discipleship. Others were surprised by how encouraging the interviews proved to be for both them and the people being interviewed. Several noted how this research process gave them confidence and conviction to pursue deeper questions and conversations on a regular basis because they noticed how natural and encouraging it felt to talk with people at a true heart level.

Overall, though we discovered that young leaders seem to be longing for personal interaction and attention perhaps even more than we anticipated. Many are not feeling cared for or invested in by other leaders and feel alone in their ministry. Therefore, it should not surprise us that youth leaders often leave youth ministry at a fairly young age because they are carrying a great deal of responsibility as unpaid young leaders. So, the clearest recommendation coming from this study is for church and Para-church leaders to focus on personal relationship and discipleship with young leaders. If we applied nothing else from this study, we could still significantly change the culture of leadership within the Czech Republic if we invested more energy and effort into caring for and discipling young leaders at a personal level.

In closing, perhaps we should take a look at the possible consequences of inaction on our part. One of the implications jumping off the pages of this study is that those who are willing to invest themselves relationally will win the hearts of future young leaders. This is perhaps as simple and intuitive as it gets. We simply can't depend on young leaders simply serving out of a sense of responsibility or duty anymore. This study shows that they are discouraged and unsure of why they are serving. We are one step away from losing them. The good news though is that we are also just one step away from raising up a whole new generation of leaders if we will be willing to invite them into our lives and care for them personally.

Proposed Experiments

In response to this study we have developed some concrete ideas and thoughts about how to address these opportunities and challenges. Our desire is that these would be simple experiments that could be tested without a great deal of investment to see what kinds of activities might bring greater potential fruit in the future. Through mutual discussion and brainstorming we came up with a couple of simple ideas.

First, to help young leaders get closer to quality ministry models, we discussed the idea of hosting a leadership round table. We would invite a group of young leaders to sit down and have an informal question and answer session with some prominent ministry leaders. This would give these young leaders not only the chance to pick their brains, but to get to know these leaders in a more personal way.

Second, we could have the more experienced leaders work with young leaders to plan a day or weekend ministry event in a specific town. Leaders and students could come together in a certain location in order spend time praying together for the city, or inviting kids to an evangelistic party. The idea behind this though is that leaders and potential leaders would be engaging in ministry together and spending time together. All kinds of opportunities for growth and informal conversations could emerge from this kind of activity.

Finally, ministry leaders within KAM could also try to become more actively involved with those whom they are leading on a personal level. Specifically, this might mean spending a couple of hours every week just meeting with youth leaders to listen, talk, and pray with those leaders. We should also be meeting with and regularly discipling a future leader (or leaders) in our own local contexts.

INTERVIEW PROTOCOLS

Czech Republic
Deep Dive Protocol

Know → Believe

How would you describe an effective leader? What are the key competencies that a leader needs to make disciples of the emerging generation? → What have you valued the most in your own development as a leader?

What have you learned about leadership in the last year? How have you learned these things? → Based on what you have learned how are you thinking differently about leadership now than you did one year ago?

In your mind, how are young people best shaped into leaders? Could you describe the process of how a young person grows into leadership? → How has your understanding of how people grow and developed made a difference in how you think about your own ministry?

Who do you know that is most effective at developing leaders? What makes them so good at raising leaders? → What do they do that you would most like to emulate if you could?

Feel → Love

What energizes or excites you about being a leader? What frustrates or drains you about being a leader? → What has kept you engaged in your leadership through the difficult or challenging periods?

What do you feel like you need to be a better leader? What do you have a strong "felt need" for? What do you sense you might need in order to grow but that you may not feel as excited about? → How has your commitment to being a leader changed or developed over the last year? What about you do you need to overcome in order to be a better leader?

As you think about the development of young leaders in your church over the next 2 years, what excites you the most? What feels most daunting? → How does the church need to grow in order to raise leaders well? What would it take for the church (or Christian community) to value and become committed to the development of leaders more?

How do young people get interested in exercising leadership and making disciples? What inspires young leaders to commit to leadership within your church? → How has your own passion for leadership development changed over the last 2 years?

Do → Become

What are you doing to help young people grow spiritually? (Describe these activities) → How are these activities changing you personally?

INTERVIEW PROTOCOL

What spiritual disciplines are you seeing people in your ministry practice today that they weren't practicing a year ago? ➞ How do you see these new practices affecting the people in your ministry in other aspects of their life? How have these shaped your own development?

What has your church done in the last year to help develop new leaders? How have you seen young leaders mature and grow in the church? ➞ What has helped you the most in who you have become as a leader?

What are some of the major challenges you are facing as you seek to develop leadership in young leaders? ➞ How are these challenges pushing you in your own growth as a leader?

In 5 years from now, if your church or denomination would grow capacity for developing leaders as much as possible, what would be your dream? What would be ideal? ➞ How would the church need to change to reach that vision? How would you need to change to reach that vision?

Estonia
Deep Dive Protocol

How did you start making disciples of young people?

Who are you disciple-making right now?

What do you do when you make disciples of others? How regular you meet with people to disciple them? ➞ How has this challenged you to grow? *(do-become)*

What are the critical elements and steps to making disciples? ➞ What does a person have to believe and value in order to become a disciplemaker? *(know-believe)*

INTERVIEW PROTOCOL

How have you been disciple and mentored by others? ➜ In your opinion, what discipleship is all about? *(know-believe)*

What difficulties have you found during discipling others? ➜ What changes need to happen in you in order to be better able to develop ministers among the emerging generation? *(do-become)*

When is a skill that you've been working on developing to make you into a more effective minister? ➜ What do you struggle with the most as you seek to grow? *(do-become)*

What are the key ministry habits that you have acquired during these past years? ➜ How has that stretched you and challenged you personally? *(do-become)*

What has been one of your greatest successes? What is your most substantial failures in making disciples? ➜ What have those revealed to you about areas where you are strong and areas that are on your growing edge? *(do-become)*

What brings you most joy as you lead and minister to others? ➜ What do you love about making disciples? *(feel-love)*

What is the sources of your frustration and irritation in ministry? ➜ What keeps you dedicated even through the difficult times? *(feel-love)*

What kinds of people or situations in ministry are particularly burdensome to you? ➜ How have you learned to move into them lovingly and as Christ would? *(feel-love)*

How has church (pastor, leadership) been supporting your work? ➜ What do you value the most about the support and involvement of your church and leadership in your own development as a leader? *(know-believe)*

INTERVIEW PROTOCOL

What is your vision for the future? If the next few years of ministry could go as well as they possible could, what would your ministry look like 2-3 years from now? → How would we in youth ministry need to grow in order to fulfill a vision like that? (do-become)

Poland
Deep Dive Protocol

What is the path to becoming an engine within youth ministry in Poland?

What do you do in ministry? What caused you to do what you are doing? → How did you come to be the kind of person who is able to reach and make disciples of youth? (DO-BECOME)

When did you realize that you were a minister? → How did you come to believe that God had a call on your life and would use you to draw young people to him? (KNOW-BELIEVE)

What did you need to learn along the way to become effective at reaching youth? → What were the breakthroughs, turning-points, or paradigm shifts that happened in your own thinking along the way? (KNOW-BELIEVE)

What or who has influenced you the most in ministry? → How has your life been shaped for the ministry? How has your life been shaped by ministry? (DO-BECOME)

What concerns you most about this generation? What gives you most hope? → How has your heart developed over time for seeing youth become followers of Christ? (FEEL-LOVE)

INTERVIEW PROTOCOL

What are your greatest fears or concerns about your ministry? ➦ What causes you to continue in ministry despite the challenges? What would help you develop an even greater love and commitment to ministry? (FEEL-LOVE)

What deflates or discourages you about ministry? ➦ When things get tough, what prevents you from giving up? What is your source of strength to keep going? (FEEL- LOVE)

What gives you most joy as you minister? ➦ How has your heart for young people grown as you've experienced ministry? (FEEL-LOVE)

What hinders your ministry? What keeps you from being even more effective in ministry? ➦ What threatens to take your vitality away from ministry and compromise you in ministry? (DO-BECOME)

What is it about you (and those you work alongside) that makes young people follow you? ➦ How have you learned to utilize your gifts for the ministry? (DO-BECOME)

In your mind, what are the keys to effective ministry? ➦ How did you come to value and emphasize these features of ministry? (KNOW-BELIEVE)

What are your greatest needs? How are you seeking to address those needs? ➦ How do you hope to grow in the next few years? (KNOW-DO-BECOME)

What is working really well right now in your ministry? ➦ How did you develop the capacity to engage people effectively? (DO-BECOME)

What is your vision for the future of this ministry? ➦ Where do you see yourself in the future? Who would you like to become in the future? What would keep you from becoming that? (KNOW-BELIEVE-BECOME)

INTERVIEW PROTOCOL

Slovakia
Deep Dive Protocol

Describe your regular day? After school activities? What about your friends, how are their days different from yours? ➜ Which part of your day is most influencing your future? Describe our ideal/perfect day? What things that you are doing are worth your effort? D - Bc

What do you read/google most? K - Bl

What do you not like about how the world works? ➜ If you would become "director of the planet", what would change? K - Bl

What is your idea of a successful life? ➜ Where are how do you see yourself when you are 30 or 40 years old? After all your life, what would you like to remain? D - Bc

Who is your role model? ➜ In what ways would you like to become more like your role model? D - Bc

Who are you friends with? What are they like? What would your friends have to do to lose your trust? ➜ If you wouldn't have this group of friends, in what ways would you be a different person? If you wouldn't have this group of friends, in what ways would they be different? D - Bc

What are your friends like? ➜ In what ways are you similar to your friends, and in what ways are you different? KvBl

In what areas of your life do older people (parents, teachers) not understand you? ➜ What do you wish they would understand about you? K - Bl

Describe the emotions you feel when you think about your home? Why? ➞ What ways/values of your family would you want to have some day in your own family and why? F - L

What are all the things that „make you really happy? What makes you angry/sad/discouraged in life? ➞ How does it show or play out in your life? F - L

What makes you feel lonely? What makes you feel disappointment? Most out of control? Jealous? Worry? Fear? ➞ How does it show in your life? How do these disappointments affect your daily life? F - L

How do you know what's right and what's wrong? ➞ What makes you have a bad conscience? K - Bl

What makes you most hopeful, most satisfied? How does this satisfy you? ➞ How do you know that this is lasting? How does this drive you? F - L

For your friends, what does it mean, to love? When do you feel loved? ➞ What does it make you desire/want in life/ seek? F - L

When do you feel you matter, that you have meaning? Kedy sa cítiš užitočný, že máš význam? Kedy necítiš nič? ➞ What would you be willing to give your life for? F - L

What do most of your classmates believe? ➞ What do you most believe in? K - Bl

Whom do you trust? ➞ What is so valuable to you that you would stand up for or fight for? F - L

INTERVIEW PROTOCOL

Slovenia
Deep Dive Protocol

1. Most people have a group of people (sometimes two or three) that they belong to and do things with. What groups are you a part of? Tell me about them, what do you do, when do you meet, where do you meet? (Note: Be prepared to change questions to past-tense – What group were you a part of?)

2. What led you to participate in this group? (Know)

3. What is your "place" or role in the group and how much influence to you have on the group? (Do)

4. What are the good qualities of the group? (Know)

5. Which of these is most important to you? (Believe)

6. What are the bad qualities of the group? (Know)

7. What do you think motivates the other participants to be a part of this group? (Know? Believe?)

8. There are other things you could be doing with your time instead of spending time with this group. What do you give up to be a part of this group? (Do)

9. What would make you most sad if you couldn't go to the group any more? (Feel) or What makes you most sad about not being a part of this group anymore?

10. If you could draw or chart out your level of commitment to/involvement with the group over a period of time what would it look like? (Love) (Note: Have them actually draw it out)

INTERVIEW PROTOCOL

11. What frustrates you or annoys you about the group? (Feel)
12. What keeps you dedicated to the group even when you face these frustrations within the group? (Love)
13. When a group spends this much time together, it is not uncommon for people to have disagreements How do people within your group handle disagreements when they come up? (Do)
14. What would you like to see changed about how this group works? (Do)
15. How do you believe you can influence what this group is becoming? (Become)
16. What helps you feel like you belong to this group? (Feel)
17. How have the relationships you have formed in the group influenced or impacted you? (Love)
18. What kinds of values do the people in your group hold? (Know)
    (Note: might need to describe the word ("values."))
19. To what level do you share the same visions or values of the group? (Believe)
20. What are the most important things you have learned because of the group? (Know)
21. How has being a part of this group affected the way you see your life and others? (Believe)
22. Who or what make it hard for you to be involved with this group? (Feel)
23. How do you respond to these influences that may try to keep you away from the group? (Do)

INTERVIEW PROTOCOL

24. How has being a part of this group influenced how you want to live and who you want to be? (Become)

25. How do you see your involvement with the group growing in the future? (Love) or What made you leave the group? Do you see yourself ever returning? What would need to happen for you to become a part again?

Ukraine
Deep Dive Protocol

What do you like best about your life these days? What do you enjoy doing? How do you spend your time every week, besides being at school and with family? How has this past year been going for you? → What are you doing that means the most to you these days?

Think back to your time at camp, what did you discover about yourself at camp? → What has been most valuable to how you view yourself now/today?

What new things did you learn about God at camp? → How did that change your thinking (perspectives) about your relationship with God?

What felt most exciting and meaningful to you during camp? → What were you most hopeful about when you left camp?

What has been the hardest for you or most discouraging about your life since camp? → How has your decision to follow Christ made a difference in how you handle the difficulties in your life?

What does it mean to be a follower of Jesus? → How has your view of God changed or developed since camp?

Camp taught us about some Christian practices—like how to read the Bible and pray and be with other Christians. What did you learn how to do that you didn't know before? → How does it affect your life now? (What do you apply to your life now?) What has been the lasting impact of camp on your life?

Life and Faith

What motivates you most in your life right now? → What causes you to be motivated by those kinds of things?

Who do you admire most? What do you admire in others? → What kind of person do you want to become?

Right now, what is the highest priority of your life? → What are your dreams for your future?

What is your biggest challenge or struggle in your life right now? → How would you want your life to be different than it is right now?

How does God fit into your life right now? How does the church fit into your life right now? → What makes you connect or disconnect from God and his people?

What is most exciting to you about your faith and walk with God? → How would you need to grow to deepen and strengthen your walk with God?

If could design what your relationship with God would be like 2 or 3 years from now, what is your ideal vision for your faith and walk with God? How can I/we encourage and pray for you in the future?

Made in the USA
Charleston, SC
27 August 2013